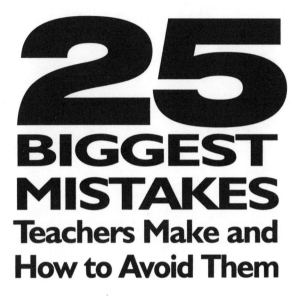

25
BIGGEST
MISTAKES
Teachers Make and
How to Avoid Them

This book is dedicated to my mother, Alma . . .
my beacon, my rock and my friend.

25 BIGGEST MISTAKES
Teachers Make and How to Avoid Them

Carolyn ORANGE

CORWIN PRESS, INC.
A Sage Publications Company
Thousand Oaks, California

For information:

Corwin Press, Inc.
A Sage Publications Company
2455 Teller Road
Thousand Oaks, California 91320
E-mail: order@corwinpress.com

Sage Publications Ltd.
6 Bonhill Street
London EC2A 4PU
United Kingdom

Sage Publications India Pvt. Ltd.
M-32 Market
Greater Kailash I
New Delhi 110 048 India

Printed in the United States of America

Library of Congress Cataloging-in-Publication Data

Orange, Carolyn.
    25 biggest mistakes teachers make and how to avoid them / by
Carolyn Orange.
        p. cm.
    Includes bibliographical references and index.
    ISBN 0-7619-7516-0 (alk. paper)
    ISBN 0-7619-7517-9 (pbk.: alk. paper)
    1. Teacher-student relationships—United States Case studies.
2. Effective teaching—United States case studies. 3. Interaction
analysis in education Case studies.   I. Title.   II. Title:
Twenty-five biggest mistakes teachers make and how to avoid them
    LB1003.O73 2000
    371.102'3—dc21   99-6838
                                                                CIP

This book is printed on acid-free paper.

00 01 02 03 04 05 06 7 6 5 4 3 2

Corwin Editorial Assistant: Julia Parnell
Production Editor: Denise Santoyo
Editorial Assistant: Cindy Bear
Typesetter: Rebecca Evans
Cover Designer: Tracy E. Miller

Contents

2. TEACHER-STUDENT RELATIONS

Preface

Teachers have power. They have the power to determine success or failure, to empower or destroy, to elevate or diminish, to enrich or deprive. Their power is embodied in what they say and don't say, what they do and don't do, what they teach and don't teach. Like any other power, if it's not controlled, it can be dangerous. Unfettered power can prey upon an unsuspecting classroom and wreak havoc on young minds and bodies. Knowledge is also power; knowledge of the difference between words that hurt and words that heal, between actions that praise and actions that diminish, between instruction that enlightens and instruction that confuses, is power. The power of teaching is inherent in the job. The power of knowledge is acquired. Knowledge can balance the power of teaching if it is expanded and used appropriately. This book proposes to expand the knowledge of appropriate discipline, student–teacher relations, instruction, assessment, policy, and teacher behavior. When teacher power runs rampant new knowledge can restore the equilibrium and restore the psychological balance that is so necessary to protect the young minds that are our charge.

Acknowledgments

The debts I owe to those who made the development of this book possible are many. These debts assume many forms, from belief in my ideas, to encouraging words, to research and editing, and to final critiques. I am indebted first, to my students who shared their experiences so candidly; then, to my editor, Jay Whitney, who believed in my idea; next, to my graduate assistants, fondly referred to as "Excellent" Emily Gaston for her typing and editing assistance and Rita "The Sleuth" Brewer for her tireless research efforts. I also must thank my daughter, Traci "eagle-eye" Hodges, who loves to edit and proof mom's papers. Thank you Claudia Brown for your editing efforts; a friend in need is a friend indeed. A special thank-you for the teachers who critiqued this work and offered their suggestions: Susan Dudley, Janet Haskins, Terry Hildebrand, and Doris Stowers. I'd like to thank my Director, Christopher Borman and my

Dean, Dwight Henderson for their support. I must take sole responsibility for any errors in content. Finally, I'd like to thank my husband and colleague, Dr. John H. Orange, for his editing assistance, encouragement, and support.
The contributions of the following reviewers are gratefully acknowledged:

Robert Stansberry
Associate Professor, University of West Florida
Pensacola, FL

Terry Hamm
Director of Special Education, Old Rochester Regional School District
Marion, MA

Joe Hoelscher
Psychologist
Amherst, OH

Margaret Borrego Brainard
Assistant Professor, Department of Educational Studies, Guilford College
Greensboro, NC

About the Author

Carolyn Orange, PhD, is Associate Professor of Educational Psychology at the University of Texas at San Antonio. She teaches Psychological Basis of Learning, Learning and Development of the School Age Child, Human Growth and Development, and Psychology of Human Motivation. She has a PhD and Master of Arts degree in Educational Psychology from Washington University and a Bachelor of Arts degree from Harris Stowe State College. She began her teaching career in the St. Louis Public Schools where she taught for a number of years. Her work as an educator has spanned about 25 years and includes some time spent working for two corporations. She has worked as a teacher, substitute teacher, consultant, researcher, and professor in a variety of educational settings: elementary, secondary, English as a second language, Montessori, special education, adult education, art, and college.

Dr. Orange has produced a video on self-regulation and has developed a Self-Regulation Inventory. She has published numerous articles in journals such as the *Journal of Adolescent and Adult Literacy, Journal of Experimental Education, The Roeper Review, Journal of Communications and Minority Issues, The NASSP: Curriculum Report Journal of Black Studies,* and *The High School Journal.* Her current research interests are envirosocial factors that affect student achievement.

Introduction

Alas, words and deeds that cut deep to the tender core of the
inner self, leave scars on the soul that can last a lifetime.

—Carolyn Orange

This bit of prose capsulizes a problem that occurs all too often in classrooms across the country. Some teachers do and say things that traumatize students, leaving them psychologically scarred from childhood on into adulthood. I use traumatize in the academic context of psychological or physiological effects that an aversive situation has on a person that results in devastating, long-term effects or lasting negative impressions.

When we reflect on our academic past, most of us can remember one or two teachers that we will never forget for a variety of reasons. For some of us it was the superstrict, no-nonsense teacher that didn't smile until Christmas, or maybe it was the kindly teacher that made each child feel special. Perhaps it was the teacher with the smile in her eyes that believed in us when we did not believe in ourselves. Or, lurking in the shadows of our reflection there is the specter of the teacher who left a lasting negative impression on us through unfair treatment, physical injury, mental cruelty, incompetence, or poor instruction.

Teachers in the latter group have left those of us unfortunate enough to cross their paths diminished in some way. Their overt and covert acts have had lasting effects that have spanned decades for some people. Many adults can remember with incredible clarity humiliating or devastating events that happened to them in second or third grade, as evidenced in the following quotes:

> " . . . This happened 33 years ago and I still remember the embarrassment."

> " . . . To this day I remember how traumatized I was and how ashamed I felt."

> " . . . The worst was that when she would yell at me, everyone laughed at me. It still hurts to remember."

> " . . . To this day, I'm still apprehensive about math."

" . . . This was her idea of an audition for the play. It was very traumatic."

". . . I still bear the scars. I haven't sung in public since that time . . ."

These quotes are excerpts from the student reflections that are the basis of this book.

The reflections are scenarios of students' worst experiences with a teacher in elementary school, high school, and college that I have collected from pre-service teachers since 1992. I have collected about 325 scenarios from pre-service teachers in St. Louis, Los Angeles, and San Antonio. I became interested in this topic when I taught a teaching laboratory. As a part of the professional development component, I asked students to recall both the best teachers they could remember, and their worst experiences with teachers. Their oral recollections were so powerful that I decided to ask for written accounts. They wrote fondly of good experiences with teachers and they showed some emotion when talking about these teachers. However, when asked to recount their worst experiences with teachers, they did so with such fervor and intense reactions, that I felt this aspect of their academic experience should not be ignored. I realized that teacher mistakes are not usually discussed or explored in teacher preparation programs.

Most education classes offer some discussion of positive classroom behaviors that enhance or create a positive physical environment, but little attention has been paid to the negative behaviors that taint the intangible, psychological environment. Teacher mistakes can wreak havoc on the intangible dimensions of classroom interactions that affect the feelings, emotions, and self-esteem of students. If one teaches, mistakes are inevitable.

All teachers make mistakes. By its very nature, a mistake is not intentional. A mistake is an uninformed strategy, an impulsive act, an unconventional discipline tactic, an inadvertent slight, a remark in jest, and the list goes on. Why do teachers make these mistakes and continue to make them year after year? They make them for many reasons. They make them because they are unaware of the impact and long-term effects of their words and actions. Teachers make mistakes because they are unaware of more appropriate strategies and techniques. Teachers make mistakes because they need to feel that they can control their classrooms. In time of crisis, they don't have a repertoire of skills to draw from, so they do what comes naturally with no thought given to long-term consequences.

I agree with Weimer (1996) that teachers learn important lessons about teaching from hands-on experience or by doing. Surely that includes making mistakes. Conceivably, teachers can learn valuable lessons from their mistakes, but if those mistakes are potentially damaging to a student either physically or psychologically, then those lessons are too costly in terms of human capital to learn by doing. Canfield (1990) reminds us that we must create classrooms that are physically and psychologically safe for all students. Therefore, it behooves us to minimize the number and type of mistakes made in teaching. As a preventive measure, it seems plausible that the scenarios in this book could provide an important teaching tool for teacher preparation classes. I think a book that addresses these mistakes will provide a useful tool of prevention and intervention for preservice teachers, practicing teachers, and others concerned with effective teaching. There are many books on positive teaching, discipline, and management, but I have yet to encounter a book that seeks to teach from the proposed "undesirable teaching" perspective offered by the scenarios.

I am writing about mistakes, not because I have never made any, but because I have learned from them. I also believe that we can learn a lot from the mistakes of others. The tone of this book is not to criticize teachers for making mistakes; instead, the purpose is to offer a way for teachers to learn lessons about teaching by learning from the mistakes of other teachers.

Bandura (1986) would call this vicarious or observational learning. Using mistakes as a teaching strategy is much like simulation—to learn important lessons a teacher does not have to actually engage in a mistake to learn from it. I recall making my share of mistakes when I started teaching elementary school. I can remember one mistake in particular where my intentions were good, but my judgement was poor. I volunteered to teach a dance class after school for my 5th graders. We were invited to perform at a neighboring high school and everyone joined in the preparations. I designed their costumes. They wore imitation leopard-skin cloth over black leotards. I added a long, wispy, thin scarf of similar material for effect. The night of the performance, I thought it would be dramatic to have the girls hold candles as they danced. It looked beautiful . . . at first. When I saw some of those scarves come dangerously close to the flames my heart skipped a beat and almost stopped. I suddenly realized that I had put my girls in danger. It was too late to stop the performance because it was almost over. I just prayed that nothing terrible would happen. Fortunately, my prayers were answered; my poor judgement did not result in physical injury to my students. I'll always remember that my students could have been seriously injured and it would have been my fault. I am sure that some of the teachers in these scenarios have similar thoughts and regrets.

This book is designed to present each reflective scenario as it was written. Each scenario is analyzed to identify the key issues and seminal problems. The Rx used in this book is an alteration of the symbol used in prescriptions; in this academic context, it means a solution for a disorder or problem (*American Heritage Dictionary*, 1992). This Rx symbol is used throughout the book to signal the analyses and solutions for the problems in the scenarios. I acknowledge that my solutions are presented with a personal bias that reflects my years of teaching, my research, my personal experiences, my readings of relevant literature, and my interactions with my students and colleagues. I concede that there are possibly other solutions to the problems presented. However, I have made every effort to present solutions that I believe are based on sound principles and appropriate practice and in most cases are supported by theory and empirical research.

As I read the reflections, patterns of mistakes seemed to emerge from the collection of scenarios. Twenty-five categories of mistakes were identified and organized into the following six sections.

Chapter 1, "Discipline," focuses on the unacceptable or inappropriate methods that some teachers resorted to when trying to control their students. There were different variations of physical aggression, alienation, and ridicule.

Chapter 2, "Teacher-Student Relations," examines interpersonal relations that involved favoritism, discrimination, personal attacks, mistreatment, humiliation, and inappropriate relations.

Chapter 3, "Classroom Policies and Practices," looks at classroom policies and toileting practices.

Chapter 4, "Classroom Management and Instruction," details the employment of a variety of inappropriate educational strategies and assessments.

Chapter 5, "Personality and Professionalism," explores personal areas such as teacher insensitivity and academic shortcomings. It also includes professional areas such as poor organization and administration, reputation, and other blatant errors.

Chapter 6, "Teaching Style and Behavior," investigates teacher bias, unethical behavior, false accusations, sexual harassment, and other inappropriate reactions.

Reflective scenarios, when used as a teaching strategy, can be effective in a variety of educational contexts. They may be particularly useful in professional development seminars, staff development workshops, and education courses. In professional development seminars, they provide real-life examples of undesirable teaching techniques, strategies, and their effects. Working through the scenarios informs students of the psychological minefields present in the intangible environment of the classroom. The solutions and recommendations literally provide them with a map to help them to successfully navigate the academic terrain. A sample staff development workshop would involve discussion, interpretation, expanding and building on scenarios, an exchange of personal experiences, and using these scenarios as an intervention or a preventive measure. A sampling of courses that could effectively incorporate reflective scenarios are: Educational Psychology, Classroom Organization and Management, Curriculum and Instruction, Academic Behavior Management, Instructional Strategies, Learning Theory and Classroom Practices, Social Foundations of Education, Sociology of Education, and Teaching Labs. In my Educational Psychology classes, students used the reflective scenarios and the accompanying analyses to identify good behaviors and strategies to use in the classroom, and behaviors and techniques that they should avoid.

The book is intended for practicing teachers, preservice teachers, professors of education, resource teachers, educational administrators, school psychologists, and counselors. I think it would be of interest to practicing teachers to make them cognizant of their overt and covert negative teaching comments and actions that could possibly have a negative impact on their students. Administrators and other teacher evaluators could benefit from this book because it would help them to recognize dysfunctional teaching practices, or the potential for them, and help them give teachers some feedback in this area. The book provides an essential tool for in-service or staff development training. It would also be useful as a prevention strategy.

My wish is that readers will view this book in the same positive spirit that it was written. My desire is that, in using this book, readers will learn from the mistakes of others and acquire some positive strategies and approaches. My hope is that this book will help more teachers become better teachers and subsequently will help more students become better adjusted, successful learners. If I can spare one child the hurt, pain, and scars that can last a lifetime, then writing this book was worthwhile.

1

DISCIPLINE

"Class, who can tell me what I have preserved in this jar?
No, it's not a pig or a baby cow...it's the last student
who got caught cheating on one of my tests!"

Mistake

1

Inappropriate
Discipline Strategies

The worst experience I had with a teacher was in the sixth grade. She wasn't a bad teacher but all the kids hated her. I don't recall her being that mean except when the kids were tormenting her. I guess that's why we didn't like her. She would get so upset that her face turned red. She would either yell at the top of her lungs or just sit there and ignore us for the entire day. Her name was Mrs. B. and now that I think back she was probably a really nice lady.

Well, the worst day was right before Christmas day. We asked her if we could sing her a song. She said yes. The song went:

> Joy to the world, Mrs. B. is dead,
> We barbecued her head.
> Don't worry 'bout the body,
> We flushed it down the potty,
> And round and round it went,
> Round and round it went.

The look on her face just killed me.

Rx: The two extreme discipline strategies used by this teacher invited the tormenting that she received. She either yelled at the top of her lungs or ignored the students for the entire day. Both behaviors signaled that the students' misbehaviors were having a profound effect on her. These extreme measures reinforced the students' behavior. After a while, they realized that no serious consequences would be forthcoming, so they continued to test the waters with this teacher.

9

Experienced teachers never raise their voices because they know that once you become a screamer, you will forever a screamer be. Experienced teachers would never ignore students for an entire day, under any circumstances. Ignoring them for a short period of time could be effective in some situations, but not in this case.

I have found that silence is much more effective for getting students' attention than screaming, especially if this is done at the beginning of the year. I would refuse to start teaching until I had their attention and then I would say politely, "Whenever you're ready." That was a very effective strategy for me. Gagne (1977) emphasized the importance of getting students' attention before teaching. I have found that keeping students engaged and moving smoothly from one assignment to the next leaves little time for them to misbehave. If students are working on meaningful assignments in an environment of mutual respect, there is little need for the acting out that is apparent in this scenario. Wise teachers would work to establish warm feelings and mutual respect. In this scenario the rapport in the classroom had deteriorated to a level bordering on total disrespect. At this point the teacher had nothing to lose. She could have laughed at the cruel little ditty, thereby dispelling any effect it was supposed to have on her. Her nonverbal behavior indicated that she was mortified, which would encourage more ditties in the future. Charles Galloway (1977) found that the nonverbal behavior of the teacher has a significant impact on the classroom atmosphere.

SCENARIO 15:
Clean in Thought, Word, and "Backtalk"

My twin sister and I were in first grade. We spoke little English and we were both in the same class. One day the teacher asked my sister a question that she was not able to understand. The teacher called her "dummy." I answered the teacher back by telling her that my sister did not understand her. The teacher felt I was talking back and she took me to the bathroom to wash my mouth with soap. I did not question her again, but I remember feeling hurt. I could not understand why she would not try to understand. We were also seated in the back of the classroom.

Rx: This worst experience scenario is like a porcupine; it has many sticky points. One point was asking a child who spoke little English a question in English and demanding that she understand. To add insult to that linguistic injury, the teacher ridiculed the child and called her "dummy." Another point was punishing the twin who was trying to explain her sister's predicament. A particularly sticky point was using an unconventional punishment for a perceived insubordination. The most damaging point was the deeply hurt feelings and the bewilderment felt by the child. This teacher's reaction and behavior suggests a bias toward non-English-speaking children. Finally, placing these children in the back of the room was, if not intentionally malicious, at the very least, thoughtless and insensitive.

Competent, mindful teachers would anticipate that non-English-speaking children in an English-only classroom might have special needs and would try to accommodate those needs. These teachers would have thanked the twin who offered an explanation rather than perceive it as "backtalk." The notion of "backtalk" suggests that the teacher thought of herself as the ultimate authority whose words and actions should not be questioned. "Backtalk" is a throwback to turn-of-the-century education, in which children were not supposed to speak unless they were spoken to. Washing out the mouth is an obsolete, old-fashioned practice of showing disapproval when a child says something that is considered improper. In this case, the child was appropriately defending her sibling and did not deserve any type of punishment. These children were apparently innocent of any wrongdoing and the pain and humiliation that they had to endure is inexcusable. Seating the children in the back of the room may not have been intentionally malicious, but the discerning professional would quickly recognize that this seating arrangement would be problematic for non-English-speaking children.

SCENARIO 18:
Nose, Toes, Anything Goes

My worst experience was in the fifth grade. My teacher, Mr. A., could not keep order in the class, so he used very extreme types of punishment. I would have to stand on my tiptoes with my nose in a circle on the blackboard for talking, or I would have to write 500 times, "I will not talk in class." I was a good student and very tenderhearted.

Rx: Mr. A. subscribed to unconventional methods of discipline. It seems that he wanted to create a truly effective deterrent to decrease the likelihood that undesirable behaviors would be repeated. His creative punishment combined physical discomfort, a difficult task, shame, and public ridicule, hoping that this combination would be effective. Mr. A. took an "anything goes" approach to discipline in which any form of punishment was acceptable if it seemed to stop behavior. The psychological consequences of this approach are apparent in the student's perception of himself as a tenderhearted person who was the recipient of extreme punishment. The student is correct. A good student should not be subjected to such treatment for the minor offense of talking. The teacher could have warned the student and given the student another chance. He could have offered free time for conversations, telling the students to hold their talk until that time. A more conventional, positive approach was desirable here.

SCENARIO 29:
Sticky Business

In the fourth grade my teacher, who was fresh out of college, put tape on my mouth because I was talking. She had asked us to stop all talking while working on our worksheets. I did not understand something and asked another student what the teacher had said. She called me up to her desk and put a huge, wide piece of tape on my mouth. I have never been more humiliated in my entire life. I hated her. All the students made fun of me after school.

Rx: New teachers who are recent graduates may become very frustrated when faced with the realities of classroom discipline. Sometimes they resort to whatever comes to mind to solve a discipline problem. This is a dangerous practice. Putting tape over a student's mouth sounds relatively harmless, but such an act could incur a number of risks. The student may be allergic to the adhesive or the teacher may risk injuring the student's skin when she pulls the tape off. The most obvious risk is to the child's self-esteem. In this case, the student was humiliated to the point that it evoked a very strong emotional reaction . . . hatred. The instructional strategy is flawed because the teacher demanded that students stop all talking while working on worksheets.

Experienced teachers would recognize a more collaborative approach that encourages talking and interaction to be more effective. These teachers would not put tape over a student's mouth for talking. They would know the importance of students' private speech for organizing their thoughts and ideas (Vygotsky, 1993).

SCENARIO 256:
Nosing Around in the Corner

The worst experience of my entire life was with my first grade teacher Mrs. S. The woman hit me on the arm or slapped me across the face at least twice a week. I received six "licks" that year as well. I was never allowed to go to recess and play. My nose was completely raw because the teacher would make me stand against a wall. She was removed from service after my mother and a few other moms went to school and complained loudly. The lady did not belong in the teaching profession.

Rx: This teacher was very physical. Her tactics exemplified the cycle that the more one uses physical punishment, the more one will *need* to use physical punishment. In addition, she appeared to be one of those female teachers who had difficulty understanding the nature of the development of young males and their typical behaviors. This is evident in the constant, repetitive punishment of this child on a daily basis. This type of physical abuse is what made it necessary for some school districts to abolish corporal punishment. If this teacher had to make a child stand against a wall everyday and miss recess, she was obviously an ineffective disciplinarian. She did not decrease the undesirable behavior.

The constancy of this child's inappropriate behavior suggests that it was behavior typical of a first grader. Experienced teachers would take a developmental approach to the child's behavior to ascertain which behaviors are typical and which ones are intentional misbehaviors. Effective teachers would help the child focus on appropriate behaviors as they work together to temper natural behaviors that are not compatible with classroom activities.

SCENARIO 257:
Sneaking a Peek

The worst experience during my school years happened when I was in first grade. I was an innocent child back then. One day, this girl was looking at my paper during a spelling test. The teacher said I had let the girl look. I ended up locked up in the coatroom. The teacher turned off the lights and left me there. That was the worst experience.

Rx: Almost daily, some teacher somewhere falsely accuses a student of some action. The pain of false accusation is compounded when the teacher acts on his or her false assumption. In this scenario, the punishment was extreme and probably traumatic for a very young child. A first grade child is very imaginative and can conjure up all sorts of terrors lurking in the dark. Leaving the child in the dark room was unconscionable.

In a situation like this, wise teachers would try to be fair and give the student the benefit of the doubt. They would instinctively know that the student may have let the other student look on her paper or the student may not have had any control over who looked on her paper. In such a case, no one should be punished if fault cannot be established. It would have been better to move the student who was looking on the other student's paper and find out if that student had some questions about the assignment.

The teacher could offer the student who was "cheating" more assistance with the assignment and thereby reduce the need to "cheat." Good teachers often circulate among students as they are working. The teacher's presence is usually an effective deterrent for would-be cheaters.

SCENARIO 292:
Water Sprites Strike

In first grade, a friend of mine taught me how to take the top part of the faucet off of the sink in the bathroom. So every bathroom break we would perform our plumbing techniques and watch the water shoot up from the top. Well, eventually, one of our cohorts told on us, and of course we were sent to the office. The principal scared us to death. He threatened and yelled, and even showed us his paddle. By the end of the event he had two terrified girls on his hands. But to make matters worse, I never told my parents about it and we had open house the very next week; therefore, it wasn't long before I was in much more trouble. Needless to say, since that first-grade experience, I have never once been sent back to the office.

Rx: The students in this scenario were threatened because they were taking the tops off faucets to see the gush of water. Erik Erikson (1963) would say that these children were showing "initiative," which is a natural part of the psychosocial development. Educators and parents are challenged at this stage of a child's development to encourage initiative and help the child understand that he or she cannot always act on their natural inclinations or tendencies. Knowledgeable professionals are aware of child development and will see that the children are showing initiative. These professionals will try to find ways that children can still show initiative, but explain to them about water damage and why they should not continue to dismantle working faucets. Resourceful teachers may find a way to rig up a faucet and let the children play with it.

Erikson (1963) warns that unhealthy resolution of a developmental crisis can affect a person later in life. Punishing children for showing initiative would be an unhealthy resolution for the initiative versus guilt crisis. There is a grain of truth in this because the adult student that wrote this scenario has never forgotten it and has never been sent to the office again.

SCENARIO 37:
Give a Hand, Get a Hand

I was in private school from kindergarten to first grade. For second grade, my parents decided I should go to public school, so off I went. The first day, I met lots of friends, but I had a problem with the teacher. I was sitting across from a girl who brought nothing with her (no paper, Big Chief, box, nothing!). So, my parents being who they were, I almost had two of everything.

The teacher left the room and told us to sit quietly. When she left, I started to divide my things and push them across my desk to the girl's. As I pushed, I got on my knees in my chair and raised up to get the things across. The teacher saw me and came up behind me and said, "Do what you just did!" I didn't understand, so she grabbed the back of my skirt, pulled me up and spanked me (more like a swat) in front of everyone.

My parents *never* spanked me, not even once. So I was pretty shocked and embarrassed. I told my mother that I was *bad, very bad*.

Rx: This caring child was trying to help another student and inadvertently disobeyed the teacher. Although she was quiet and semi-sitting, the teacher saw this as a blatant disregard for her instructions. The teacher assumed she knew what the student was "doing" and her expectations led her to believe that punishment was in order.

Discerning teachers try to dig deeper and go below the surface of a problem, recognizing that things are not always as they appear. In this case, the teacher should have asked the child what she was doing before she decided to punish her. Instead, she said, "Do what you just did!" and obviously her mind was already made up. Good teachers ask questions first and take action later. Having the child ask for permission to share her supplies with the less fortunate child could have been humiliating for the child with no supplies. In this case, the teacher could have thanked the child for her expression of kindness and let the incident pass. Correction of every misbehavior is not necessary (Irving & Martin, 1982).

SCENARIOS 49, 99, & 252:
Knuckle Whackers

Scenario 49

I remember having to sit in the dunce chair and getting my knuckles whacked by Sister A. for talking. I thought I was going to die.

Scenario 99

We had gotten our first homework assignment and we needed to return it the next day. I went home, did it, and my mother and I put it on my desk so I wouldn't forget it. I forgot it. When it came time to turn the homework in, I pretended like I turned it in. The teacher went through the papers and marked each child that had brought one in. At the end, a little boy and I were left with no mark next to our name. When she asked where my homework was I told her I did it but forgot it at home. She told me she didn't like me telling lies and to go over to her desk. She slapped my hand with a wooden ruler; it left paint on my hand. My friend tried to comfort me as I cried and told me not to worry because all those teachers were mean. For the first time I realized that the teacher was African American.

Scenario 252

Sister M. was my first grade teacher in Catholic school. She was very strict and mean and I was so scared of her. She used to discipline her students by hitting their knuckles with a ruler. I was one of those students.

Rx: Hitting students on their knuckles is a destructive practice that fosters anger, hatred, fear and resentment. It may also be illegal. Corporal punishment in any form is banned in 21 states. Whacking knuckles can be very painful for young children. Curiously, all of these young students were in first grade. In addition to the pain, the damage to students' dignity and self-esteem may be great. This form of discipline may change the student's perception of the teacher, causing them to see her as mean or scary. In one scenario, race became an issue; it was not an issue prior to the punishment. Exemplary teachers know how to discipline and keep the student's dignity and self-esteem in tact. Dunce chairs and knuckle whacking are turn-of-the-century discipline tactics that should be abandoned.

SCENARIO 83:
The Line-Up

In first grade, the class had a few students who were being silly (giggling, talking, etc.). Mrs. G. (I'll never forget her name) made the entire class line up in front of the blackboard and she paddled every one of us. I was totally embarrassed and furious that I was treated so unfairly by someone I trusted.

Rx: This teacher paddled her students, which is now illegal in some school districts. A more significant sin was her global use of punishment where she punished the guilty and the innocent. I also question the nature of the punishment in light of the "crimes." Giggling and talking do not merit paddling.

Wise professionals would never punish the innocent, even at the risk of letting some of the guilty ones get away with the offense. If the teacher cannot easily discern the culprits, justice is better served by dropping the matter or offering a stern warning. If the behavior continues, they try rewarding the students who are not misbehaving, which avoids giving attention to the offending students. If punishment is needed, it should be appropriate for talking and giggling. Sometimes, giving the students five to ten minutes to giggle and talk might eliminate the need for punishment.

SCENARIO 212:
Attila the Nun

I had a nun in third grade who was very old, very impatient, and probably should not have had much to do with children. I got in trouble for talking. First she called me to the front of the class and hit my hands, then she put duct tape over my mouth, and cut off some of my hair.

Rx: This form of punishment is so unconventional that it borders on pathological. What kind of behavior change would cutting a child's hair effect? The extreme, bizarre nature of the punishment suggests a very authoritarian climate. Sprinthall, Sprinthall, and Oja (1994) point out that an authoritarian approach to discipline does not permit any deviation from a strict discipline policy. This is a very antiquated approach to discipline that is very reminiscent of the "hickory stick" era.

The informed teacher would have a repertoire of procedures and consequences that are appropriate for the offense and that consider the age of the child. This teacher had a repertoire of consequences but they were all inappropriate and unconventional. A more contemporary approach would be to recognize the child's need and right to talk sometimes and to accept that talking can be a good thing.

SCENARIO 68:
Injustice and Punishment for All

I was in the fourth grade. Several students had to stay after school because we had gotten in trouble during the day for various reasons. (What the reasons were, I don't remember.) We had to write "I will not. . ." sentences. Some girls were whispering and the teacher added more sentences, then someone rolled their eyes and she added more, then someone groaned and she added more. I remember thinking what a mean and uncaring person she was. As far as I can remember, none of the students liked her, she was my worst teacher.

Rx: This scenario is a classic example of the disadvantages of group consequences. In this scenario, a number of students were detained after school to write repetitive sentences. They were punished as a group for the misbehavior of various members of the group. They had no control over these students' actions so they should not have received any punishment for acts they did not commit.

The insightful, caring professional would recognize the pitfalls of group consequences and use them sparingly if at all. Groups should not endure punishment because of an individual or individuals over whom they have no control (Epanchin, Townsend, & Stoddard, 1994). The teacher should only have assigned extra writing to those students who were causing problems. I have known teachers who have assigned extra tasks to the group not because they were mean and uncaring but more because of impulse and a desire to "control" the group. Assigning group consequences requires a serious, thoughtful approach. The risk involved in using this approach is being perceived as mean and uncaring and of being unfair to some students.

SCENARIOS 115 & 139:
Dubious Misdeeds

Scenario 115

When I was in fifth grade, I don't remember what I was doing wrong, probably talking, and the teacher made me move my desk away from the rest of the class. After I moved my desk, I put my head down and cried and cried. I remember my classmates trying to console me.

Scenario 139

The worst experience I ever had with a teacher was in the sixth grade. Her name was Mrs. H. She was very big and scary. I do not even remember what I did, I was probably talking. She took me outside and yelled at me. It was right before Thanksgiving. I remember telling everyone she wanted to eat me as her Thanksgiving turkey. I do not think I had ever been so scared.

Rx: In both of these scenarios, the students seemed unaware of their offenses and assumed that the punishments were for talking. The problem here is that neither teacher made either student aware of their offense and then did not connect the offense to an appropriate consequence. Both teachers reacted in an impulsive, hostile manner, which is ineffective.

Effective teachers would like to decrease the likelihood that unacceptable behaviors will continue and increase the likelihood that acceptable behaviors will continue. The ABCs (antecedents→ behaviors→consequences) of Behavioral Learning Theory (Skinner, 1950) suggest that behaviors should be connected to consequences to determine if that behavior will occur again . If the consequences are good, the behavior is likely to occur again. If the consequences are not good, the behavior is not likely to occur again.

Lee and Marlene Canter (1992) would probably agree that the problem in both of these scenarios is a teacher-owned problem. They suggest using assertive discipline to deal with these types of problems. If assertive discipline were viewed through a lens of Behavioral Learning Theory, the "ABCs" of assertive discipline would be as follows:

(A=antecedents) Teachers establish rules, give clear explanations of the rules and teach students how to behave appropriately. (B=behavior) Students make choices about following the rules and if they don't follow the rules, (C=consequences) assertive teachers follow through with appropriate consequences. They warn against passive or hostile consequences. If children choose to break the rules, they should be reminded of the rules and asked what they would do differently next time. This question forces children to think about what they have done, what they should have done, and what they will do next time. Assertive discipline would have been very appropriate for both of these scenarios.

SCENARIO 196:
Pay Attention!!!

In third grade, I had a teacher who yelled at me. We were having some type of quiz and we were only supposed to have one sheet of paper. I don't remember if I didn't have any or if I just decided not to listen. I used a pad of paper. When she saw that, she squatted down right in front of my desk and yelled right in front of my face. I was so humiliated. I still remember I just put my face real close to my paper and cried.

Rx: The student in this scenario was obviously distracted or not paying attention. The "crime" was not following directions. Bending down and yelling in front of the student's face was an authoritarian tactic that meant "do as I say." This teacher seems to have had a need to be in control and took the child's inattentiveness personally.

Knowledgeable teachers would know that it is not unusual for students, and adults, to become distracted in a group setting where they are forced to pay attention. Armed with that knowledge, the teacher can be patient and understanding and repeat the instructions in a civil tone. Some students need to hear the directions for an assignment more than once. If the students still do not understand after one or two repetitions, the teacher could demonstrate or have class members explain the assignment in their own words until everyone understands. Before giving instructions it is always advisable for a teacher to wait until she has everyone's attention.

She should model the instructions as much as possible using the actual materials. If not paying attention had been a pattern with this student, the teacher could have let the student know, before the instructions were given, that the student would be expected to help by repeating the instructions to the class.

SCENARIO 194:
Cheating Exposé

I was in middle school and I was caught cheating. The teacher took up my paper and asked, in front of the class, if I thought that it [cheating] was worth it.

Rx: The teacher exposed a cheater in class. On the surface, this seems reasonable. The teacher's intent seemed to be to embarrass the child enough that this cheating behavior would cease.

Insightful, experienced teachers know that students cheat when they do not know the material or they are afraid that they do not know enough of the material. Sometimes, students feel pressure from parents and high-achieving siblings or peers to do well in school. Thus, the motive for cheating becomes an important issue. If teachers are aware of the cheating motive, they can help students with the problem, effectively eliminating the need to cheat. A public exposé could cut off any means of communication. A soft reprimand in private would be more effective (O'Leary, Kaufman, Kass, & Drabman, 1970). In private, the teacher is more likely to get an explanation. Issuing a referral for cheating should be a last resort.

SCENARIO 169:
Biting in Self-Defense

My fifth grade teacher made me apologize to another student for biting her. The other girl was trying to take my shoes away and I had no other resort. We were in the restroom, and she was much bigger than I was. She ran to tell the teacher, and I was forced to apologize. What I did wrong was that I did not give my side of the story because she had no reason to take my shoes.

Rx: Conflicts among students often escalate into violence. Studies have shown that most conflicts among students are usually not effectively resolved (DeCecco & Richards, 1974). In this scenario, the teacher did not manage student conflict appropriately. She listened to one child and in a perfunctory manner, she made the wrong child apologize. She did not bother to find out what happened.

Resourceful practitioners would ask both children what had happened. If both students insisted that the other was wrong and the conflict could not be re-solved, they would use peer mediators to help the students settle their dispute (Johnson, Johnson, Dudley, Ward, & Magnuson, 1995). They would not arbitrarily decide that one student was right and the other was wrong.

SCENARIO 170: No Apology Needed

My second grade teacher was Mrs. M. I remember that the girl behind me was not behaving correctly. She was talking when the teacher was teaching. So the teacher got mad. She got up and went towards the girl, but before she got to her she hit my shoulder, then she grabbed the girl and shook her. I was surprised but scared. Every time we saw Mrs. M. we were quiet. I remember telling my mom. My mother went to talk to the teacher, but the teacher denied everything.

Rx: Anger is a breeding ground for inappropriate actions. In an irate attempt to discipline a student, the teacher accidentally hit the wrong student, an innocent bystander. The teacher failed to acknowledge her mistake and she later denied it ever happened, which only added insult to the child's injury. There are a variety of reasons that the teacher failed to acknowledge her mistake. She was oblivious because of her rage. Sometimes angry people want to hold on to their anger, and stopping to apologize would diffuse the anger. Another reason could be that the teacher did not feel it was necessary to apologize because she was the teacher and the student was just a student. Perhaps there are more reasons, but whatever they are, they do not justify the teacher's actions.

Any reasonable human being would stop to apologize and say "excuse me." If a teacher is too angry to do that, she may be putting too much of herself into controlling student behavior. Such anger can push a teacher across that reasonable, litigious line separating appropriate and inappropriate discipline. The professional teacher with integrity would admit her mistake, and thereby eliminate any need to lie to parents to cover it up.

SCENARIOS 107 & 130:
No Explanations, Please

Scenario 107

In the second grade I received a paddling for pinching a classmate. The classmate and I had made a bet to see who could pinch each other the hardest. I took my pinch. When I pinched her she started crying and I got in trouble. I thought we both should have gotten in trouble because she pinched me too, but I didn't cry.

Scenario 130

It was kindergarten, my first day, and boy, was I in trouble. I was all tomboy and very used to being in charge. I punched a boy who was continuously picking on me and my friends. Well, I hit him so hard he fell over and began screaming. Here comes Mrs. M. "Who did this?" "I did, but he. . ." "That's enough. We are going to have to call your mother." So I sat in a chair in the corner scared to death until my mom came. From that day forward I remembered the "look" that my teacher had given me. Did I do it again? Well, not in kindergarten—not until first grade. Even now twenty years later when I see her she still gives me that "look."

Rx: In both of these worst experience scenarios, the teachers did not bother to ask for explanations or to hear both sides of the story. In these cases, justice is blinded by a lack of explanation and no consideration of circumstances. Such an authoritarian approach to discipline leaves no room for clarification, explanation, or illumination.

Diplomatic professionals, who exercise sensitivity in dealing with all children, would listen to both sides of each story without hesitation. If they still feel that punishment is necessary, they would make sure that it is meted out fairly. This may mean that both children will be disciplined, rather than just one.

SCENARIO 89:
Whodunit?

In kindergarten the teacher paddled me for sitting at a table where one of the girls called the other girl fatso. However, the teacher didn't even ask if we had, she just took the girl's word and paddled all of us because we were at the table.

Rx: The teacher was not monitoring the students' behavior as they sat at the table. She could not possibly know who actually committed the "offense." Additionally, calling names is not acceptable but scarcely warrants paddling.

It was inappropriate for the teacher to take one student's word over another, considering she did not know who was guilty. Resourceful practitioners would use this situation to discuss the hurtful effects of name-calling and suggest that the students show some empathy for the victim. Punishment is out of the question because the teacher does not know whom to punish. The teacher could begin by offering the students an apology and by admonishing the act in general. She could model a more prosocial approach by making a positive comment about the student. Empathy facilitates prosocial behaviors (Ormrod, 1998).

SCENARIOS 143 & 176:
Sitting Ducks

Scenario 143

My math teacher in elementary school was calling on me. I didn't hear him. To wake me up he threw a piece of chalk at me.

Scenario 176

Ms. G. would throw erasers in class, hit students, and call students stupid and ignorant. She was very old and very crabby. She grabbed my arm once and it turned black and blue. My mom went to the school and complained to the principal.

Rx: Throwing objects at students can be a very dangerous practice. The projectile can miss its mark and cause serious injury. Although the teacher may choose something soft like a chalkboard eraser, as the object gains momentum, the impact may sting a little. Whatever the object, the teacher runs the risk of damaging a sensitive area like a student's eye. When I was teaching fifth grade, a colleague often used rulers to make angry gestures at her students to try and get them to sit down or stop talking. In one tragic incident, the ruler slipped out of her hand and accidentally hit a student in the eye. One of my elementary school teachers would throw erasers at students in the classroom. He prided himself on the element of surprise. I lived in fear of being the target of one of his erasers. It was a very ineffective technique. The unruly students thrived off the attention and the orderly students withdrew in apprehension.

In the current classroom environment, astute teachers have to learn to

Perceptive, responsible teachers assess their share of the problem and take action. They would begin by finding ways to improve instruction and by ascertaining alternate approaches to helping students. Effective teachers would focus their efforts on helping students improve their performance, which would eliminate the need for disparaging remarks and angry outbursts (Sabers, Cushing, & Berliner, 1991). Shaping (Skinner, 1987) is a behavioral strategy that effective teachers use often. Using shaping, teachers reinforce successive approximations or small steps of progress toward a specific behavioral outcome and offer praise and encouragement at each step. For example, they could praise the fact that the student brought in the homework, next praise the neatness of some of the letters, next, note that the paper does not have erasures, and so on. The child will most likely try harder to get some praise and approval and is less likely to try harder for hurtful remarks.

SCENARIO 7:
Ready, Willing, and Able

My worst experience with a teacher is one where I was singled out without my permission to "help" a student with dyslexia. I didn't mind helping at first, but the experience turned into one where I did all the work and the teacher did none and neither did the other student. I felt unappreciated and felt that the situation was unfair.

Rx: Peer tutoring has its merits, provided the tutor is willing and able to provide quality instruction. In this case, the child assigned to be a peer tutor was neither willing nor able. This child did not "agree" to tutor the student and this child was not trained to teach students with learning disabilities. The teacher passing the total responsibility for teaching the dyslexic student on to a resentful child compounds this problem. Apparently the dyslexic student sensed the teacher's abandonment and the tutor's frustration and opted out of that educational process.

Peer tutoring has been shown to benefit the tutor and the tutee (Good & Brophy, 1997). Teachers should only use peer tutoring if it is mutually beneficial to both students. Student tutors should be willing participants and should not be expected to work beyond their level of mastery. Caution should be exercised with students needing tutoring to avoid making them feel "less than" for needing assistance.

SCENARIO 245:
Talk, Talk, Talk

My worst experience with a teacher was in eighth grade at St. L.'s School. Her name was Mrs. D. Even as an eighth grade student I realized that she was a bad teacher, the worksheet queen, Ms. Boring!! She taught her class in the lecture style all year long and half the time I had no idea what she was talking about. She never smiled and never tried to make any connections with her students.

Rx: Lecture can be an appropriate teaching strategy, but this strategy should be reserved for students at the high school level and above. The younger the students, the more disengaged they become as time goes on. If lecture is used, it should be interesting and include as much media as possible. Integrating video, audio tapes, visual aids, PowerPoint-type computer presentations, CD-ROM, and other sensory sources will keep students engaged and will enhance the effectiveness of lecture as a teaching strategy. Kindsvatter, Wilen, and Ishler (1988) suggest three ways to enhance the lecture presentation: use visual aids, present simple material before complex material, and use nonverbal behaviors to hold students' attention. This teacher missed the mark on all three points. She used worksheets, a less desirable instructional tool, she used no visual aids, and she presented complex material most of the time. She never smiled. This simple nonverbal expression would have helped her to connect with her students and to minimize the gap that seemed to emerge from her ineffective use of the lecture method.

A more effective approach is articulated in the concept of connected teaching, proposed by Belenky, Clinchy, Goldberger, and Tarule (1986). They suggest that connected teachers function as a midwife that helps students give birth to their own ideas as opposed to functioning like a banker who merely makes knowledge deposits in a student's head.

SCENARIO 298:
Here an "F," There an "F," Everywhere an "F," "F"

My single worst experience in school was my high school economics teacher. I had this teacher my last semester during my senior year. On the first day I had his class, he stood in the middle of the classroom and proceeded to tell us how he prided himself on failing students. From that moment on, I knew I was in trouble. He gave us two chapters to read every night and would lecture over things not in the book. His tests were hard because nobody ever knew what he would test us over. I had a horrible time making him happy with my projects. In the end, after working very hard, I made a B in the class.

Rx: There is a degree of irony in the pride this economics teacher takes in failing students. Little does he realize that failing a large number of students is a direct reflection of the inadequacy of his teaching. He entertains the misconceived notion that the goal of education is to fail students. His deliberate attempt to fail students is apparent in his practice of not communicating the objectives of his instruction to students and not relating his tests to these objectives.

Effective teachers would make every effort to avoid failing a student. There are a variety of strategies available to teachers to avert failure, such as providing cues, encouraging students, and offering multiple exposures to the material and multiple opportunities to learn the material presented.

Effective teachers would try to make sure that students understood what is expected of them. They would provide specific instructional objectives for students that would help students to direct their study efforts to meet the teacher's goals and objectives. Gronlund (1995) recommends objectives that focus on student behaviors and learning outcomes.

SCENARIO 310:
Academic "Payday"

In 1985, I moved to San Antonio from Houston. The school placed me in an advanced math class. Though honors math wasn't new to me, I found the class learning aspects of math that I had never been introduced to. I fell behind. Feeling frustrated, I approached my teacher on several occasions for help. However, she never made time for me. Within six weeks, I was failing and felt demoralized. The school chose to put me in an average math class. On my last day, I told my teacher that I would ace the quiz. She said, "I doubt it." Well, I earned a 100. I showed it to her, left, and never spoke to her again. In case you're wondering, I made all As in my new math class.

While in the end, I believe that I came out triumphant, I find it a very negative memory. In my opinion, no one is permitted to doubt my ability. Not even me.

Rx: This teacher missed her "payday" by failing to find time to help a student. Teachers often derive a psychic income from helping students who truly need help. In this scenario, the student's failing grade spawned a vengeful motive for achievement that was conceived in hostility and resentment. It would have been so much easier and productive to help the student or to provide help for the student. There are many help venues available such as computer-assisted instruction, tutors, peer-tutors, or one-on-one instruction. This teacher could have been a beacon of light for this student; instead, she became a lasting negative memory. This lost opportunity was truly her loss.

SCENARIO 151: If at First You Don't Succeed, Try, Try Again, and Again, and Again

I was a very sensitive child, easily hurt. Probably the worst times with teachers were when I felt ostracized or made a spectacle of. Sometimes teachers would have no regard for how much they can embarrass a child in front of his peers.

One particular time when I was in eighth grade PE class (the worst year of my life). We were practicing batting the softball. The teacher had us line up and each had to stay until we hit the ball. Everyone else hit it after a few tries, but I had to stand there and swing and keep missing. After about ten to fifteen tries, he let me pass. That class was also bad for letting the kids pick teams. I was, all through school, the last one picked. I will never intentionally let that happen to a child.

Rx: This student sums up the problem in his statement that some teachers "have no regard for how much they can embarrass a child in front of his peers." This teacher crossed the boundaries of reasonableness when he forced this child to keep trying to hit the ball for an excessive number of tries with no apparent hope for success. The child obviously did not have the skill set to hit the ball. This teacher crossed the boundaries of decency when he made an example and spectacle of this child and allowed the classmates to witness the agonizing event.

Effective teachers would set a reasonable limit on the number of attempts students would be allowed to make before they could pass. If a child cannot perform after several tries, teachers, as trained professionals, should diagnose students' weaknesses and re-teach those skills until the students succeed.

Physical education classes are notorious for creating anxiety by fostering the anxiety that accompanies "picking teams." Insightful teachers can anticipate the stress and anxiety that students who are at the bottom of the pick list will feel. If teachers used a lottery system or a similar method of selection to assign teams, the stress level would be significantly reduced, if not eliminated.

Mistake
15

Inappropriate Assessment

My worst experience was starting private school in sixth grade and being told that I should repeat fifth grade based on some test scores. Later I found out I had been given the wrong form of a test so I didn't have to repeat fifth grade.

Rx: The teachers in this test situation made a serious error that could have resulted in misplacement, stigma, and retarded academic development if the student had to repeat the fifth grade.

Prudent teachers know that placement of students should not rely on one test score. Glaser and Silver (1994) contend that testing has become separated from instruction. Messick (1984) says that testing should be a last resort and quality of instruction should be a primary concern. If it appears that the classroom performance is average and the test score is low, give students the option of moving up to the next grade level or repeating the grade. In this scenario, there was no mention of class performance so it is difficult to determine if instructional outcomes were taken into consideration. The quality of instruction should be considered before a student is tagged, labeled, and shipped off to a lower grade.

SCENARIO 153:
"F": Feedback or Folly?

In eighth grade my English teacher was awful! She hated me. I would do a paper and get a F. I even had a certified teacher, who was our neighbor, help me on one paper. I still received a F. We changed teachers for one six-week term, and I received an A that time. My parents finally had me transferred to his class, so I could have a chance to pass. I ended up with As in his class, where I had made Fs in her class. I did nothing different. I can honestly say it was just a personality conflict. I guess there was something she did not like about me. I know I will do my best to never let myself be influenced like that so that I would fail a student. I hope to be fair to all of them and will strive hard to achieve that goal.

Rx: Teachers who wield a big sword with an F on it intend to hurt someone. They are no longer evaluating grades; they are carrying out a vendetta of unknown origin. Perhaps as a child, this teacher felt the sting of getting an F, maybe even an undeserved F. Knowing the power of the failure, perhaps this teacher was identifying with her oppressor when she consistently gave Fs to a student she disliked. She effectively used the bad grade as a weapon.

Emotion is often a barrier to effective student assessment. Some teachers allow their personal feelings about students' academic potential, attitudes and beliefs, personal appearance, social class, race, or gender to bias their grading or assessment. Teacher bias seems apparent in this scenario but the factors underlying the bias are not clear. When a teacher's assessment of a student embraces bias, the grades or scores are useless; they only reflect the inaccuracy of bias and offer no meaningful feedback on student achievement. The inaccuracy of biased grading is evident in this scenario where the student consistently made Fs in one class and made As upon transferring to another class. The disparity in grading is a red flag that perhaps the student was right. The teacher probably disliked the student and tried to use grades as a punishment.

Fair-minded teachers have high expectations for all students. They are aware of their responsibility to set appropriate achievement goals for all students, including students they dislike. Delivering quality feedback is virtually impossible in the presence of bias. Using appropriate assessment to identify student needs allows teachers to target instruction to address those needs, which effectively enhances the achievement of all students, particularly low achievers (O'Connor, 1998).

Informed teachers realize that the purpose of assessment is to provide quality feedback that can be used to improve student performance. They know that a grade of F is only a form of feedback. They also realize that using grades for punitive reasons is pure folly that is doomed to end in failure for the student. . . and the teacher!

SCENARIO 96:
I Am Not My Brother's Keeper

When I was a senior in high school we were taking our exit tests. We were placed three at a table in the library to take our tests. The day we got our results back, the boy who sat at my table came up to me with his score. He told me he was so relieved that he passed because he had copied all of my answers and then found out we probably had different test forms. Luckily for him we didn't, so he passed his test and graduated because of me. When I complained to the counselor and they said they couldn't do anything, I flattened his tires!

Rx: Improper management of a testing session permitted a student to cheat and capitalize on another student's scores. Experienced teachers use preventive measures and adequate proctoring to discourage cheating. Preventive measures include but are not limited to using parallel forms of the test, spacing students to make it difficult for them to see each other's tests, scrambling test questions and creating corresponding answer keys, or giving scrambled electronic versions of the test. Wise teachers know that proximity is often a deterrent to cheating. Frequent proctoring and scanning the room should minimize or stop cheating activity.

SCENARIO 228:
Caustic Critique

I was a freshman in college, and I thought I had made it. I wanted to be a writer, and I thought I could. I had been given so much positive reinforcement in high school. I felt on top of the world. I handed in my first English paper to professor P. (I'll never forget his name). I anticipated greatness. As he handed my paper back, I flipped to the back page, anxiously awaiting the glorious comments. The simple red print asked, "Is English your first language?"

Rx: This scenario has two possible angles: the student was deficient in self-evaluative techniques and the teacher was deficient in effective assessment techniques, or the student was a good writer and the teacher was a sadistic critic. In the first instance, the student possibly had an overinflated sense of her writing ability and the teacher's grade was justified but the comment was unduly harsh and disparaging. In the second instance, the grade was undeserved and the comment disparaging. The consequences of a disparagement model of assessment are many. Foremost, a personal attack on the student's competence directs the attention away from legitimate concerns about the manuscript to personal characteristics of the author. This tactic contributes nothing toward the improvement of the manuscript. In fact, a personal attack may close the mind of the recipient, destroy the writer's confidence, and discourage aspirations of being a writer.

Encouraging educators would instinctively know that sarcasm and ridicule are not effective for improving student performance. In lieu of the disparagement model, they would opt for a germination model of assessment where the topic is the seed and the stu-dents' first attempts at writing are viewed as the planting of the seed. Teacher feedback on specific errors and strategies for improvement help to cultivate and weed the growing seed. Helpful comments and suggestions water the seed. Encouragement and praise provide the sunshine. Rewrites of the paper simulate stages of germination. A finished paper that is well written is the blossom of the endeavor. A caustic critique can nip the germination process in the bud.

SCENARIO 180:
Being Taught Red-Handed

In third grade our teacher Miss Y. decided to give us a quiz on our multiplication tables. The day before the test she told us that if we didn't make a 100, we would get a spanking (with a yardstick) on our hands. So of course I was upset and nervous. The day after the quiz Miss Y. went up and down the rows. When she came up to me all I got was my paper with a grade of 100 percent. I was relieved but upset because some children actually got the spankings in front of the whole class.

Rx: The multiplication assessment in this scenario is reminiscent of the Gestapo tactics of old. In this case, having 100% on the quiz was the equivalent of having "papers." Going row by row and systematically spanking those who did not have 100% may be likened to stopping people to ask for their papers and arresting or punishing those that did not have them. Some of the teacher's misconceptions that are apparent here are that threats of punishment can guarantee outcomes or that assessment should be used to determine who needs punishment. The teacher seems unaware that assessment can be used to determine who needs remediation.

The teacher's terroristic tactics polluted the classroom climate with stress and anxiety that possibly affected everyone. The student in this scenario reported being relieved but upset because the class had to watch the children get spankings. The class probably experienced the spankings vicariously. The pressure to perform and the potential for punishment also contribute stress and anxiety to the classroom climate. Wigfield and Eccles (1989) warn of the perils of this combination.

Knowledgeable teachers know that assessment should provide feedback for students in need of remediation. These teachers know that using fear and punishment as a motivator is not as effective as using remediation, praise, and encouragement. They also recognize that having students compete with themselves and strive for improvement is much more effective than giving students one shot at a perfect score and punishment if they miss. Good teachers are cognizant that the quality of instruction may be a factor when students miss learning goals. They evaluate their instruction and re-teach concepts if necessary. They realize that spanking has no role in the improvement of instruction. On the contrary, it has more potential for injury. Students need remediation, not punishment.

SCENARIO 290:
Group Consequences: All or Nothing

In my senior year in high school, I had a group project in my sociology class. When the time came for our group to present our findings, one of our group members didn't show up. The teacher proceeded to tell us that we would all get zeros on the project. I then burst out of the room, went to the principal's office, and waited to see the principal. I was not going to allow my teacher to give me a zero. My teacher walks in and starts to scream at me for walking out of the class. I was humiliated, but we got an extension on our project.

Rx: The potential for unfairness and inequity is an implicit problem in the assessment of group projects. In some instances, one student does all of the work and in some instances one or more students do very little or no work. Assessment becomes problematic when students' grades are contingent on the work of other students. The teacher had a rigid, high stakes, all-or-nothing grading policy. All students had to be present for anyone to get a grade. It was not apparent that the teacher had communicated these grading criteria to students in advance because they seemed surprised by it.

Understandably, such a rigid, unfair policy precipitated a number of undesirable consequences. One of the students was vehemently opposed to the teacher's grading practice. The student's anger was possibly rooted in a fear of the impact of the grade of zero on being able to graduate. The teacher had a tangential tantrum about the student walking out of class but seemed oblivious to the looming fairness issue.

Proficient educators establish guidelines for group assessment in advance and make students aware of their criteria for grading. They realize the importance of basing individual grades on individual effort. Grades are not contingent on the performance of others. Perhaps a separate grade evaluates group effort and collaboration, but students are not penalized for criteria that are beyond their control. Effective teachers are mindful that students' grades should reflect their attainment of instructional objectives. They encourage students to do self-evaluation to become more self-regulating (Stiggins, 1994). They know that peer models are useful for teaching self-evaluation and other self-regulatory skills (Orange, in press). These teachers model good evaluation when they grade fairly and follow these guidelines.

SCENARIO 101:
Inflexible, Indifferent, Illogical, and Inaccurate

In third grade math we took a test. I had all the answers correct, but I missed a space on the test so all my answers were off. The teacher placed me in the "lower" math group. She did not listen to me when I tried to explain what happened.

Rx: There are a number of assessment-related problems embedded in this scenario. One is using a single test score to place students in groups. This practice has many flaws, one of which is incorrect placement, as depicted in this scenario. The teacher's indifference to the student's mistake resulted in an illogical placement and inaccurate feedback. Such an inflexible environment leaves little room for students to make an error.

Clifford (1990) posits that the assessment environment should be conducive to risk-taking and freedom to make mistakes without undue penalty. Astute teachers avoid the one-shot opportunity that discourages risk-taking and opt for a more flexible form of assessment that allows students to make some mistakes with minimal, if any, penalty. An environment where students are not allowed to make mistakes impedes learning and hinders critical thinking. Good teachers may give practice tests or bonus questions to allow mistakes without penalty. If a student makes a simple error on a significant test, experienced teachers consider helping students to reconcile the mistake and obtain their actual score. In this scenario, the student had all the correct answers in the wrong places. Helping the student make the correct placement is more important than penalizing the student for the mistake. Moreover, the effective teacher is aware of the ills of ability grouping and is wary of placing a student in a low group using one criterion, a test score, even if it is a standardized test. There are a variety of forms of assessment that could supplement a test score and help teachers make a more informed decision if they insisted on grouping by ability.

SCENARIO 161:
Tragedy on the Classroom Stage

In my senior year of high school, I had to take either band or theatre arts to be the first valedictorian to graduate under the advanced diploma plan. I chose theatre arts even though I was shy and really dreaded it. I asked the teacher for exemption from the Christmas play for religious reasons. (She seemed to take this personally.) During the many weeks preparing for the play, the only thing I was asked to do one day was go to the local craft store and get some materials. One Wednesday she told everyone that they would have a dress rehearsal. Well, I didn't think that applied to me because she had me stuck off behind her when she said it, plus the fact she never gave me anything to do. So I didn't go. I went to church. My best friend tried to call me when she arrived and found out I was going to get a zero for not being there. She actually had to lie to the teacher and sneak across the street because the teacher wouldn't let her call me. (She didn't reach me.)

The next morning, I was in history class and the principal came and got me. I couldn't imagine what was going on because I was never in trouble. When we got to his office, the teacher was there and she started literally screaming at me for not going to her practice. She then told me that she had given me specific duties to do when in fact she had not. She gave me a zero with no way of making it up. I was devastated.

Rx: This scenario had the makings of a tragedy rooted in religious drama from the beginning. The setting is a dreaded drama class that the student is forced to take. Next, she opted out of the play for religious reasons. Her shyness may also have influenced her decision. The teacher was not pleased, possibly because the play was a major part of the grade. The student seemed to think the teacher took her exemption from the play personally. The plot thickens, as the student is truly exempt from the production because she has no specific duties or responsibilities. The turning point in the story is when the student skips dress rehearsal because of some miscommunication about her role in the rehearsal. The cliffhanger is that a friend tries to warn her of the impending danger of getting a zero, but the teacher will not let her. BOO. HISS. The teacher emerges as the villain, going after the student with a vengeance. She enlists the help of the administration to bring in the student. Foul play and suffering is heaped upon the student as the screaming teacher lies about the student's duties. In a moment of high drama, the teacher gets her revenge by giving the student a zero with no opportunity to make it up. The student endures the suffering and accepts her tragic lot. Tragically, she may not have made valedictorian. She is doomed to remember and relive this event for many years.

Discerning teachers would suspect that fear and shyness were protagonists in this classroom drama. These teachers would have alternative duties and ways of assessing the performance of a shy student. They would also respect the student's religious decision and offer an alternative assessment. These experienced teachers would inform the student of expectations, specific alternative responsibilities, and grading criteria in advance. There would be no reason to use grades to punish the student because there would be no misunderstanding. A potential tragedy would become an ordinary classroom performance with the potential of a happy ending.

5

PERSONALITY AND PROFESSIONALISM

"Looks aren't everything. It's what's inside you
that really matters. A biology teacher told me that."

Mistake

16

Teacher Insensitivity

SCENARIO 13:
Seeing Red

My English teacher offered to help students with their papers before they handed them in. As a student eager to do well, I went to her for help. She basically destroyed the essay as well as my self-confidence in my writing. I can still vividly see my introduction crossed out in red. I had spent so long working on it that to see it all rejected felt horrible. While she was supposedly trying to help me rewrite it, more of her ideas and words were going down on the paper. I can't remember her exact words, but I know for years afterwards, I had horrible writer's block. It took me several years to accept the idea that I might be a good writer. I still can't put words and sentences down unless I think they are perfect. Additionally, since then, I have never asked a teacher for help with a paper.

Rx: Traditionally, red ink was used in accounting procedures to record debits and losses. Perhaps educators borrowed from this practice and used red ink to grade student papers to note deficiencies and mistakes. The practice of using red ink for grading has been so overused and misused that red ink has become symbolic with failure. When students see returned papers covered with red ink, they often see red. After their anger subsides, they are left with diminished self-confidence and fear of failure or of making mistakes.

Some teachers, like the one in this scenario, are insensitive to the effect red ink has on students. Although her intent was to help the student, the teacher in this scenario was not sensitive to the student's reaction to the grading. It seems suspect that so much of the student's paper was crossed out in red.

Effective teachers know that they need to clearly state the objectives and expectations for the assignment. Brophy (1982), attributed some student failure to a lack of clarity about what they're supposed to be doing for the assignment.

Good teachers know the importance of balancing criticisms with positives. They praise student effort and hard work as they make suggestions for improvements.

Skilled teachers avoid imposing their words and ideas on students. Instead, they encourage students to critically evaluate their own work and edit and revise it as needed. This helps students to appropriately attribute their successes and failures (Weiner, 1979). An alternative is for both the teacher and the student to edit and critique the paper, then compare their edits. If there are any discrepancies in the edits, the student is responsible for using references to look them up and determine which is correct. Finally, a good way to keep students from seeing red is to use other colors to grade papers, such as green or purple.

SCENARIO 4:
And the "Winner" Is . . .

My worst experience with a teacher came when I was in junior high, and there was an awards ceremony in PE. All the students in three classes were sitting in the bleachers, and the three PE teachers were down on the gym floor. They would call each student receiving an award individually to come down to receive their ribbon, certificate, letter, etc. I was never good at sports, so I knew my name would not be called. I was very surprised when I heard, ". . . and the next award goes to (my name)." The award was for "BIGGEST PHYSICAL RETARD."

They meant this to be funny. I have no actual physical disabilities. All the students laughed. I tried to take it in good humor, but I felt humiliated. My adult perspective is that it's a terrible idea to make fun of an adolescent in public. Even if the child knows that it is a joke, no big attention should be made that is derogatory—especially in front of a large group!

Rx: Award ceremonies are usually held to recognize student for their accomplishments. At award ceremonies, there is usually an air of goodwill and anticipation, as students wait to see if they have won something. When students win, emotions are high and joy prevails. When students lose, hope often informs the determination to do better next time. When students are ridiculed for their efforts, hope becomes humiliation and pain prevails.

The insensitive coaches had no regard for the student's well being. They all had a good, hearty laugh at the student's expense. Students have a difficult time in school when they are different in any way. In this case, maybe the student had poor coordination or a physical problem. Whatever the reason, it did not warrant the humiliation of a student under the guise of a gag award. To make matters worse, the student felt compelled to laugh with the crowd to conceal the depth of her pain.

Good teachers would only use an award ceremony for that which it was intended . . . to recognize achievement.

They would never use the ceremony as a forum for humiliation and shame. Woolfolk (1998) decries anything that draws attention to a student's physical differences, which includes physical performance. Instead of looking at a student's effort as half bad, it is more helpful and productive to view it as half good. An award that recognizes effort is much better than a nonproductive attempt at humor.

SCENARIO 77:
Name Sweet Name

In third grade I was adopted and my last name changed during the middle of the year from M. C. to M. B. My teacher refused to change my name. I was so excited to be adopted by my stepfather and it deeply upset me that she would not acknowledge it. She insisted on calling me by the wrong last name.

Rx: The adoptive process is centered on the welfare of the child—the physical and psychological welfare. Adoption obviously boosted this student's self-esteem and sense of belonging. Having a new last name was symbolic of the love and acceptance she had been granted. The teacher threw cold water on her happiness by refusing to acknowledge her new name. It's difficult to determine if the teacher's inaction was rooted in malice or ignorance. There is no excuse for either.

Insightful teachers would sense the feelings of happiness and pride that being adopted gave this student. They would make a conscious effort to remember the new name. Many teachers would take the opportunity to help the child celebrate the new name by reintroducing her to the class, using her adopted name. Another way to acknowledge the student would be to put the child's picture on the wall with the new name underneath and the word "congratulations" over the picture. These acknowledgements should only be done with the child's permission.

SCENARIO 42:
Exit Front and Center Stage

In first grade I had an accident in class during naptime and the teacher made it obvious. I sat in the back of class. There was a back door out of the room, but she made me first sop up my mess with paper towels, then leave the room out the front with the wastebasket to go to the principal's office.

Rx: The problem in this scenario is that the teacher treated a young child's accident as if it was a misdemeanor that warranted shame and public exhibition. Having the child clean up the mess, carry the trash can containing the soggy mess, and, as a finale, take the trash can out of the front door was a demeaning, covert form of punishment.

The insensitive teacher had no empathy for the child and made a conscious effort to make the situation obvious. Perhaps the motive for this less than empathetic response was that the teacher felt she could not let the accident go unnoticed because it may encourage others to do the same.

Empathic teachers would respond to the child's accident with minimal attention and class interruption. They would send for the janitor to do a quick clean up while they directed their students' attention to other relevant instructional matters. Students would learn the valuable lesson that accidents happen and maintaining dignity is a better approach to handling an accident than invoking shame. Children should not be sent to center stage for unintentional acts of behavior that are better known as accidents.

SCENARIO 84:
Eye to Swollen Eye

My PE teacher completely ignored me when I told her my eye was bitten by an ant and was swollen. By the time I got back to regular class, my eye was swollen shut and I couldn't see. The main thing I was mad about was that she completely ignored me and didn't even look at me.

Rx: The teacher in this scenario didn't bother to look at a student who was complaining of an eye injury. This reckless act of indifference could have endangered the injured student. If the teacher had at least made eye contact, she could have readily seen that the student's eye was swelling rapidly. The student could have had an allergic reaction or serious injury to the eye. Prompt attention to an injury is necessary to protect the well being of the child. This teacher's lack of response borders on negligence.

Prudent teachers investigate all student complaints of injury immediately. Although some complaints may be trivial, to ignore them may risk ignoring a serious or life-threatening injury. Sometimes just acknowledging students' injuries makes them feel better. It's human nature to want to tell someone where it hurts. Good teachers are willing to listen.

SCENARIO 93:
Diagnosis: Faking

My worst experience was in the fourth grade. My teacher made fun of me and called me names like "baby" because I was very sick with migraine headaches. She would accuse me of faking just to go home. I used to cry all the time, especially when I was sick, because I was scared. I never ever faked. To this day, I am a migraine headache sufferer and I go through a lot of treatments that include daily medicine, therapy, and Demerol. But that teacher was the poorest excuse for a teacher that I ever had. My mother was furious and had a real long, LOUD talk with her one day and then she changed her ways.

Rx: The unsympathetic, insensitive teacher in this scenario is not trained to diagnose illnesses, but she presumed to diagnose faking an illness. She taunted and ridiculed a sick child because she thought the child just wanted to go home. She labeled the child a baby because the child cried about her illness. Migraine is a serious illness that involves headaches, severe pain, and visual disturbances. The severity of the migraine varies by individual. For a fourth-grader, intense pain and visual disturbances can be very scary.

Sensitive, compassionate teachers would respect the student's illness, show concern and offer assistance. Teachers should never assume that a student is not ill. If they don't want to take the student's word for it, they should request doctor's statements or other documentation to verify the illness. Consulting parents about the legitimacy of the illness is a good alternative.

I am a lucky migraine sufferer. I have migraines with visual disturbances but without the pain. They began when I was a sophomore in college. It was very scary for me and I was an adult. Good teachers know that illness is scary, and they make efforts to calm students and to make them more comfortable.

SCENARIO 98:
When the Bough Cracks

I was sick and had ulcers. I went to class and I had to get up and leave the classroom. I felt ill and knew I was going to be sick. When I got up and was walking towards the door my teacher chased me out and yelled at me for leaving. He embarrassed me in front of everybody. I told him I was sick and going to the bathroom. He just turned around and said he was going to mark me absent.

Rx: The new green twig on the branch of a tree is full of life, supple and yielding as it bends to withstand the winds of change. In contrast, the dead, dry twig is hard, unyielding, unbending, often cracking under the forces of change and nonconformity. In many ways, the teacher in this scenario is like the dead, dry twig. He is hard and callused in his attempt to punish a sick child. When the sick student breaks the rules by abruptly attempting to leave the classroom, the teacher turns a deaf ear to the student's explanation. The teacher finally cracks and starts yelling and chasing the student. His cracked, irrational behavior shatters the peace of the classroom. His punitive action has embarrassed the student, created an inaccurate attendance record that could cost the school some dollars, and encouraged truancy.

Like the green twig, reasonable teachers easily bend and sway with change. If there is a change in routine or a disruption in class because a student is ill, these teachers skillfully handle the emergency without losing momentum. They would keep the disruption to a minimum by giving some gesture of approval to assure the student that leaving is permissible. Caring teachers would follow up to make sure the student was feeling better or to provide further assistance. They are flexible and willing to relax the rules in times of crisis.

SCENARIO 172:
The Bereaved Must Leave

When I was in fourth grade, my grandmother had just passed away. Since we were very close, that was a difficult time for me. I would cry in class sometimes when I began to think about her. One day I was crying, and Ms. H. sent me out into the hall.

Rx: Bereavement is a state of loss of a loved one. Grief is the overwhelming feeling of anguish or sorrow that accompanies bereavement. Crying is a natural expression of that grief. Children and adults cry over the loss of loved ones. Crying is therapeutic for some people. If crying is so natural, healthy and therapeutic, why is the teacher so bothered by it? The teacher's discomfort with the child's display of grief may be attributed to the conventions of our society. A public display of grief, outside of funerals, is viewed as disconcerting and sometimes inappropriate. As a society we are uncomfortable with tears. We are quick to offer a tissue to sop them and stop them. Sending the child to the hall for crying was an insensitive act that may give a child the impression that she had done something wrong.

Compassionate teachers are tolerant of tears. If a child is crying these teachers feel compelled to investigate the cause of the crying and to offer comfort if necessary. Gelman (1983) contends that people should be allowed to work through their grief. Understandably, teachers might have a problem with crying if it disturbs the class too much. They might involve a counselor or social worker when the child needs to cry. Resourceful teachers would seize the occurrence as an opportunity to discuss bereavement, grief, and expressions of grief. Caring teachers may be tempted to touch or hug a crying child. Teachers, if they must hug, should know that they do so at their own risk. An alternative would be to have a volunteer hugger or a close friend of the student offer comfort. This may be effective for young children. Explaining the nature of grief and providing comfort for the student could reduce a potentially disruptive occurrence down to a minimal distraction.

SCENARIO 109:
Children Must Be Seen and Heard

When I look back at grade school and think about my worst experience, Mrs. P. immediately comes into my mind. She was the PE coach, and I always thought she was so mean. One day in PE class, I was talking too much, well at least in Mrs. P.'s eyes I was. To be honest, I do not even remember if I was talking a lot that day, I was always so quiet and never got in trouble. After PE class that day, Mrs. P. told me, "A., you have not shut your mouth today at all!"

As I walked away, I was so hurt and wanted to cry. What hurt even more was when my third grade (and all-time favorite) teacher told me that Mrs. P. said I misbehaved that day. I admired Mrs. B. so much. She was so disappointed in me, and I will never forget that day.

I hope that one day I will meet Mrs. P., and let her know that I am going to be an elementary teacher very soon, and that I have learned and experienced so much. PE class should allow young children to be free and expressive to a certain extent. I do not think talking should be punished with such harsh and personal words. They could remain with a child for a lifetime. I can still hear her voice so well in my head, even today. I lived through the experience, but it scares me to think of the other little kids who will not live through it.

Rx: The last part of the student's scenario is a fine response to the first part. He is about to join the ranks of good teachers who would agree with him. Young children should be free and expressive in classes like art, physical education, and music classes.

Mistake

17

Academic Shortcomings

My worst experience with a teacher was my first grade teacher. She sent me to the corner and didn't allow me to be a helper (chalkboard cleaner) because I could not write my name correctly. I was devastated and felt ashamed of my incompetence. I also was extremely nervous the remainder of the year.

Rx: This teacher is confused in her assumption that "not learning" is a punishable offense to be punctuated by shame and deprivation. According to information processing theory, several exposures and repetitions of material are necessary to encode information into long-term memory (Woolfolk, 1998). Good teachers know that some young children have more difficulty learning skills and concepts than others do. They are aware that cognitive development varies in children (Piaget, 1952) so they expect variation in children's classroom performance. There are so many traditional and innovative ways to help children learn to write their names that punishment need never have been an option. Effective teachers are aware that shame is not an effective motivator. Competent teachers would have used some writing readiness activities or some one-on-one instruction to help their students practice. They would try not to discourage their students by shaming them. Instead, these teachers would empower their students by praising their efforts and inspiring them to do better the next time.

When I was in second grade I had a problem with two young boys that were in another class. During my PE class they would throw rocks at me. One day I told my teacher what they were doing and she did not believe me. She told me to stop acting like a baby and she did nothing to help me out.

Rx: In biblical times stoning, or throwing rocks at a person, was an act of violence that was used to kill someone. Although the students' rock throwing is on a smaller scale, it is still an act of violence. The teacher ducked her responsibility in the rock-throwing incident and blamed the victim. Her lack of action sent some negative messages and paved the way for some serious consequences.

One negative message was that the student was unimportant and not worthy of protection. The teacher's indifference added psychological insult to the victim's physical injuries. The teacher's indifference sent a message to the young men that there were no consequences for their violent, antisocial actions. This message has serious potential consequences for the young males. By successfully participating in minor misbehaviors, they may get the impression that it's acceptable to engage in inappropriate behavior. Kauffman (1989) found that boys are more likely to be discipline problems than girls are. Ignoring the young boys' behavior places them at risk for engaging in more serious delinquent or criminal actions.

Although the teacher managed to duck the rock-throwing incident, she might have had a little more difficulty ducking a lawsuit if the young men had injured the student. The school has a responsibility to protect students by preventing or punishing serious discipline problems. The teacher placed herself, the school, the victim, and the perpetrators in jeopardy by ignoring this act of violence.

Sensible teachers act on misbehavior immediately. Gottfredson (1984) stressed the importance of communicating to students that they must obey school rules. Otherwise, schools run the risk of communicating to errant students that misbehavior is sanctioned. Responsible teachers know it's important to act immediately, before misbehavior escalates into delinquency. Good teachers try to prevent misbehavior; they punish inappropriate behaviors and get parents involved as much as possible. Creative teachers can find ways of teaching prosocial behaviors that effectively diminish antisocial behaviors.

When I was teaching elementary school and students hurt other students, they had to apologize and make their victim feel better. I would have them wipe their victim's tears, get their victim a drink of water, and in some cases, rub the child's hand and ask if he or she felt better. Most of the time the both students would end up smiling or laughing. Sometimes I would make the perpetrator the victim's protector for the rest of the day. I tried to do this in a humorous way. It worked for me. Sometimes students would give their own genuine apology and they would play together at recess.

Years ago I visited a classroom that had a rule posted that said, "Hands are for hugging and for loving." I was really impressed with the prosocial message in this rule. My hope is that more teachers will adopt prosocial rules for their classroom that extends beyond the traditional "don't do this and don't do that."

SCENARIO 3:
A Know-a-Little and a Know-It-All

I cannot pinpoint a specific negative experience. The general ideas that come to mind include a teacher who did not know her content area as well as I did as a student. We often had arguments about answers that I would win. Another teacher told students they were "misguided and wrong" if they did not agree with his interpretations of history.

Rx: Some above average students have an overinflated sense of what they think they know. In some cases they're not teachable because they think they know more than the teacher knows. On the other hand, sometimes these students are correct; sometimes they do know more than the teacher knows about the content area. Some teachers have an overinflated sense of what they know about their subject and fail to adequately prepare for their lessons. I was supervising a student teacher who found herself in the embarrassing predicament of not knowing some fifth grade math. She informed me later that she was so sure that fifth grade math would be easy that she didn't bother to prepare for the lesson.

Wise teachers seldom take content for granted. If they have been teaching for awhile, they know that content may reflect new developments, techniques, concepts, and understandings. Most teachers know that nothing is constant but change and that it pays off in instructional dividends to be prepared. Advanced preparation of lessons helps teachers pinpoint areas of weakness before they present the information to students. Resourceful teachers make pro-

ductive use of this advanced warning to correct any deficiencies that are apparent.

The second example in this scenario features a very authoritarian approach to instruction. The teacher seems to think he's all-knowing and students are misguided and wrong if they don't agree with him. Constructivist teachers know that it's important to help students to construct their own meaning to make sense of the world (Anderson, 1989). They are aware that it's difficult to do that if they discount their students' contributions. These teachers realize they must let students have a voice and a choice in instructional matters. Belenky et al. (1986) suggests that teachers learn to trust and respect each student's experience. Wise teachers attach value to their students' responses and interpretations although they might not agree with them. Good teachers want their students to become more self-regulated learners, which means they are willing to become less involved in lessons and become more of a facilitator of learning. These teachers encourage students to participate more in their own learning, and to assume responsibility for what they learn and to rely on the teacher less.

SCENARIO 203:
Academic Inquisition

One of the experiences that happened to me in grade school was during Halloween. Trying to act like my mom (who is a Jehovah's Witness) I went to school and did not participate in the Halloween party. My teacher asked me why and I explained that my mom doesn't celebrate the holidays. The teacher phoned my mom to tell her my position and when I got home my mom did not say it was good or bad which was very confusing for me. I wasn't mad at the teacher, just confused.

Rx: One definition of inquisition is an investigation that violates the privacy or rights of individuals (*American Heritage Dictionary*, 1992). This kind of activity dates back to the thirteenth century when the Roman Catholic Church used inquisition to combat heresy (*Concise Columbia Encyclopedia*, 1995). This teacher's actions are reminiscent of the actions of the old tribunal. She dared to question and interfere with a student's religious preferences. Calling the mother about the mother's religion and her son's choice was clearly a violation of the family's privacy.

Sensitive teachers respect a student's religion and culture. If students choose to adopt their parents' religion, which is often the case, teachers should respect that choice. It seemed that the mother did not try to impose her religion on her child, which possibly explains why the mother had nothing to say about the child's decision. The mother appeared to respect her child's right to choose and the teacher should do no less.

SCENARIO 76:
Jumping to a Gender-Biased Conclusion

I was in fourth grade and in all of the "A" group classes. I made As in everything except math, but got thrown into "honors" math because I was in this group. I remember making a failing grade on a test. When my mother went to parent-teacher conferences, the teacher had us sit in with our parents. My mom asked her what she could do to help me and the teacher said, "Nothing, she is just not a math person and will never be." To this day I have a phobia of math!

Rx: "Never" is such an absolute term. Imagine a child hearing that she is "not a math person and will never be." Such a label of hopelessness could easily become a self-fulfilling prophecy (Rosenthal & Jacobson, 1968). Why would a female teacher make such a disparaging remark about a young girl? One guess is that she may be echoing comments that were once made to her or her female classmates. If she is unaware of the gender bias in math classes against girls, she may see nothing wrong with her comments. When I was in high school, I can remember a math teacher saying to me, "You should never take any more math classes, you're too careless." I internalized this opinion and I freely told people that I was not very good in math. I only took the required math courses in my undergraduate studies. I only aspired to a C because, after all, I wasn't very good at math. I nurtured this belief until I applied for graduate school. I froze when I saw that statistics was a required course. I was very upset when I realized I couldn't get through the educational psychology degree plan without taking that statistics course. Fortunately, I had a great professor, Dr. Linda Stewart, who was a visionary. She was aware of mathematical gender bias long before the study that revealed that girls were often shortchanged by schools (AAUW, 1992). She encouraged me to enroll in the program and wait for her to teach the statistics course. She already knew that I had been told I was not suitable for math and had been advised not to take any more math

courses. She assured me that I would do well in her course because she had a systematic way of teaching that makes it easier for women. I received an A in statistics and I was elated, not so much because of the grade, but because I could dispel the myth that I wasn't good in math. I regained my confidence, but I was one of the lucky ones. There are many young girls that never regain their confidence, as evidenced by the author of this scenario.

The first step toward eliminating bias is to become aware of it. Encouraging teachers are necessary to imbue young girls with the confidence they need to take more math courses. The American Association of University Women (1992) found that boys have better math scores than girls on the SAT. They attributed that discrepancy to girls taking fewer math classes rather than a lack of ability. Maple and Stage (1991) found that girls are now taking more math classes and the gender gap on math scores is closing.

Good teachers never say never, especially when trying to predict a student's success in an area. Possible is a better word than never; it's a word that fosters hope. We can empower students by telling them that anything is possible.

SCENARIOS 21 & 69:
Tread Lightly, But Do Tread

Scenario 21

All through school I was always labeled as a hyper child so I labeled myself as a hyper child who had a hard time in school and it was not till I was twenty-two years old I was discovered as being ADD. It really frustrates me still today that my disability was not discovered until two years ago! However, I am dealing with it and for the first time in college, I made an A on a test with the help of Ritalin and last semester I got a 2.0—the closest I have ever gotten to a 3.0.

Another experience was my junior year in high school and I was in Advanced Geometry, the first advanced class I ever attempted and I was studying with my mom and my boyfriend, C. After turning the homework in, C. and I both missed the same problems and he was a straight A, advanced student and I was a B, C, regular student and she called me a cheater!

Scenario 69

In third grade I visited the orthodontist over Christmas vacation and was fitted for a retainer. Anyone who has experienced this knows it can be humiliating, especially in the speech department. It takes some getting used to. When school resumed I was still having some difficulty. My teacher, obviously hoping to be awarded "teacher of the year" for noticing this defect, placed me with a speech pathologist.

Rx: Trying to determine if a student has a learning disability or a physical disability is a difficult, sensitive process. Teachers should tread lightly in these areas, being careful not to misdiagnose, but tread they must, lest they miss a diagnosis or condition. Scenario 69 is a misdiagnosis. The teacher jumped to the erroneous conclusion that the student had speech difficulties and remanded the student to a speech pathologist without further investigation. If she had treaded lightly and talked to the student first or obtained further evidence of a problem, she could have avoided misdiagnosing the student. The teacher does deserve credit for trying to act on the student's behalf.

Scenario 21 is a case of missed diagnosis. For about twenty years, no one suspected the student had attention deficit disorder. This disorder is making its way to the forefront of research on exceptional learners, as increased knowledge of the disorder becomes available.

Diagnosing attention deficit disorder (ADD) may be difficult because it mimics attention problems in other disorders (Slavin, 1994) and in some cases, children may have difficulty paying attention and not have ADD or any other disorder.

To avoid missing a diagnosis of a disorder or misdiagnosing a disorder, effective teachers will proactively arm themselves with knowledge. They learn how to identify learning disabilities according to their school district's rules, regulations, and requirements. They learn characteristics of students with learning disabilities or physical challenges. They become knowledgeable of the legal ramifications of serving exceptional learners. Effective teachers tread lightly in recommending students for special education to avoid contributing to the disproportionate number of males and African Americans that are overrepresented in special education (U.S. Department of Education, 1991).

SCENARIO 126:
All Talk and No Teaching

My worst experience with a teacher occurred with my dance instructor my senior year. She taught the dance class the dance team was required to take. I was the colonel of the team and therefore had to work very closely with the teacher. It was her first year at the high school; however, she had been a teacher for another Texas school for two years before. She was totally unprofessional with her job. Days that we were to practice a dance routine for competition, she would sit the whole team down and explain how her house was haunted with ghosts. She wanted to be everyone's friend instead of teacher. She was eventually fired about three-fourths of the way through the year. Being that I was the colonel, an unbelievable amount of stress and responsibility was placed on me. I should have been paid for doing her job. There are so many stories I could tell you that you wouldn't even believe. It's really sad when I look back to my senior year as being the worst. I truly believe that if I hadn't gone through what I did, I would have gone on to become a professional dancer. This teacher just took my will to dance and crushed it.

Rx: A favorite source of recreation for many students is to get the teacher to go off on the proverbial tangent, in other words, to digress from the subject matter. Students find it more difficult to get experienced, prepared teachers to digress. This teacher was inexperienced and obviously unprepared. She presented very little challenge to students; as a matter of fact, she made it very easy for students to deviate from the subject matter. She totally abdicated her responsibilities as a teacher to talk about ghosts in her home. Perhaps she wanted to entertain her students, or there is always the possibility that she was mentally disturbed. Whatever the problem, she was not functioning as a competent teacher. She shifted her responsibilities to her student assistant. Her student suffered much psychological harm as a result.

Competent teachers know that first and foremost, they should put their students' instructional needs before their own personal needs. Most teachers like to interact with their students. They are well aware that teachers should be friendly but not necessarily the students' friend. Effective teachers will entertain their students occasionally but they realize that entertainment is no substitute for structure, organization, and quality instruction. These teachers will have instructional objectives that will keep them focused on the lesson and make it harder for students to distract them or direct them to some tangential topic. Finally, most conscientious teachers do their own teaching and rarely shift that responsibility to a student.

SCENARIO 234:
Don't Know Fall From Autumn

My worst experience was in kindergarten. I was asked, "What are the four seasons?" I replied, "Winter, Spring, Summer, Fall." The teacher said, "No, it's not Fall, it's Autumn." I was mortified and never went back. I wouldn't tell my mother why I was so upset. It's a wonder I learned to enjoy school when I started first grade the next year!

Rx: The student had a rather extreme reaction to the teacher correcting the student's response to the question. Perhaps it was because the teacher's "correct" answer was incorrect. Apparently, the teacher wasn't aware that autumn and fall are used interchangeably. In the dictionary, autumn means fall (*American Heritage Dictionary*, 1992). If the teacher was aware that they were the same, she didn't have to embarrass the student to express her preference.

Experienced teachers would not have missed the opportunity to let the child know that fall is also referred to as autumn. However, those teachers would be savvy enough to praise the student's response first and introduce the idea of autumn as a bit of extra information. An idea-friendly environment would encourage meaningful exchange of information between students and teachers. Students should be encouraged to give added information when it is appropriate. This scenario should encourage teachers to proceed with caution when correcting students with such absolute certainty. Good teachers are prepared to admit they are wrong if they make a mistake, or if they are not sure an answer is correct, they put it on hold until they can research it.

SCENARIO 145:
Teaching Solo: Students Can't Hear You

I was in tenth grade. I had this teacher that was from somewhere else other than the United States. She always wore long sleeves and a long dress or pants. She also wore a scarf over her head. Her whole body was covered. Anyway, she had no control in the classroom. Everyone was always loud and she would teach from an overhead and talk so softly that no one could hear her. I did not learn geometry at all that semester. To this day I have a lot of trouble with it. She just did not know how to teach well.

Rx: Effective communication is a critical component of effective instruction. How can students learn if they can't hear the lesson? Students can't hear if the class is disorderly. Judging from the student's account, the teacher had no control of her class. Her soft-spoken attempt at instruction was rejected by the students, as evidenced by the disorder and chaos and the lack of participation in the educational process. This teacher was truly teaching solo. She lost her students when she opened her mouth and nothing came out but whispers and snatches of academic information.

Experienced teachers would use what's commonly referred to in academe as the "teacher voice." Developing this voice is an art that requires practice. A good teacher voice is audible, clear, purposeful, commanding, and can usually project across the room. Skilled teachers know that using the teacher voice appropriately minimizes discipline problems and effectively enhances instruction. Voice inflection, volume, tone, and accent will help communicate the teacher's messages and desires to the students. Expert teachers are able to use their voices to command student attention and to communicate a no-nonsense approach to their lessons.

SCENARIO 162:
The Incarceration of Originality

The worst experience ever with a teacher was in kindergarten when a substitute teacher asked me to color a worksheet that had a witch on it. I decided to color my witch orange. After I had finished coloring my picture I proudly went to show it to my substitute and she proceeded to tell me how ugly it was and that witches were supposed to be black, so she made me color it over in black.

Rx: Primary students are known to make nontraditional uses of color in their artwork. The proud student did some creative coloring and tried to share it with a teacher. Under the guise of a mindless art critic, the teacher assaulted the child's competence and incarcerated her originality. She forced the student to change the bright orange witch to traditional black. She committed the ultimate sin of artistic evaluation: she called the student's artwork ugly.

Diplomatic teachers know that it's considered ill mannered and in bad taste to call an adult artist's work ugly, so why say that to a child? These teachers know that beauty and ugliness are both in the eye of the beholder. Teachers who seek to inspire budding artists celebrate their freshness, creativity, and originality. They limit their criticism of children's work because a budding Picasso may be among these children. Torrance (1972) found that teachers' judgement of children's artwork was not necessarily a good indicator of the creativity these children exhibited later in life. Astute teachers seek to foster creativity and encourage originality. They will encourage students to go where their vision takes them. These teachers embrace nonconformity and are amenable to divergence. Caring teachers seek to ignite and sustain the creative spark in all students.

Mistake

18

Poor Administration

My worst memory of school was in high school, my sophomore year. That year I joined the drill team because the instructor said they were going to change the image by using dancers and better costumes. So they hired a guy to choreograph the dances and design the costumes. Well, the dances were just awful and when the first game came to be, no one had seen our costumes. At the first game, the guy gave us our costumes just before we were supposed to go on. Those costumes were ugly and didn't fit anyone. The smallest one they could find to put on me still had to be wrapped around me three or four times. Everyone was so embarrassed that we thought we were going to die.

Rx: The drill team instructor did not live up to the students' expectations. Perhaps he thought the dances and costumes were fine, but he did not have to wear them and perform in front of the crowd. The entire operation seemed poorly orchestrated. There was no evidence of planning or preparation.

Experienced teachers know the value of planning. A lack of planning makes the outcome a product of chance, vulnerable to random happenings. Efficient instructors would not wait until the night of the performance to give students their costumes. They would order the costumes early enough to allow ample time for several fittings. An added benefit would be to allow students to vote on several designs before costumes are ordered. This same approach should be used for the dances. Student input would boost morale and possibly improve the quality of the dances. Finally, instructors should not make promises that they cannot or do not intend to fulfill. In this case the outcome was terrible. The instructor should have owned the mistake and given students the option of wearing the costumes or wearing something else. Forcing students to wear ugly, ill-fitting costumes at the last moment, leaving them no choice, undermines the instructor's credibility and sense of integrity.

Mistake

19

Teacher Reputation

SCENARIO 146:
Fearsome Reputations Often Precede People

The worst experience with a teacher that I can remember was in sixth grade. This was the first year that I had more than two teachers so I was already intimidated. She was my math teacher. She was known to be very mean. I never even spoke to her one-on-one, but just her looks and reputation made me tremble. Being in her class was so hard because I was afraid to even move. I felt if I moved she would see me and give me a bad look. Some kids in the class loved to make her scream and turn all red. I wanted to have nothing to do with her. The simple fear of being in her class made it so stressful that this was my worst experience.

Rx: Teachers' reputations are developed by the characteristics or traits ascribed to them by their students and peers. Their reputation is based on how they teach, how they grade, and how they interact with their students and peers. Most teachers behave in consistent ways with each class. Eventually a pattern of behaviors, expectations, and reactions becomes evident and becomes a general estimation of the teacher. Reputations can be good or bad. Teachers' reputations usually precede them, especially if the reputation is bad. The academic grapevine is a fact of student life. Students warn each other about teachers and offer recommendations of who to take and who to avoid if they have a choice.

The teacher in this scenario had developed the reputation that she was intimidating or someone to be feared because she was very mean. The teacher's reputation and looks filled the student with fear and debilitating stress. The teacher's screaming and raging behavior compounded the student's fear. It is very difficult for a student to learn under these conditions.

A variety of factors may be responsible for the teacher behaviors that precipitate a bad reputation. In classroom management courses, pre-service teachers are taught not to smile before Christmas.

Teachers who follow this advice may be perceived as mean. Pre-service teachers are encouraged to use voice and demeanor to prevent discipline problems. They run the risk of intimidating some of their students. When teachers have low expectations of students, they may treat these students poorly and gain a bad reputation from their actions. Teacher burnout is another factor. Unfortunately, some teachers who have a reputation for being bad teachers may, in fact, be bad teachers.

Effective teachers usually develop a reputation for being approachable, fair, consistent, good teachers, and good co-workers. They usually have high standards and expectations for their students.

Good teachers who discover they have a bad reputation can work to develop a warm, supportive environment that fosters mutual trust and respect. These efforts should dispel students' fears. Ormrod (1998) suggests creating an environment where students feel free to take academic risks. Stress management courses would be very useful for teachers who feel they are suffering from teacher burnout.

Mistake

20

Teacher Misjudgment

SCENARIO 208:
Shrinking Violet or Conceited Prima Donna?

When I was in sixth grade we were to do some sort of assignment that required us to stand in front of the class and speak. I was a very shy person at that point in my life and when I jokingly told my teacher I was scared of doing the assignment because I was scared, she told me that it wasn't fear, it was conceit. I felt so dumb and hurt that she thought I was conceited. I was in student council and sometimes did have to speak in front of the school, and I was in choir, so I suppose audiences shouldn't have intimidated me. However, in speaking to them I had a written dialogue that was not my own creation and I never stood alone, but technically I was still scared not CONCEITED!

Rx: The teacher erroneously confused a student's shyness with conceit. Her misdiagnosis may be based on her definition of shyness. By its very nature, shyness suggests a focus on or an awareness of self, whereas conceit suggests a preoccupation with self. However, there are many factors that influence a student's tendency toward shyness. Fear is a legitimate factor. Fear of failure, fear of success, fear of strangers, fear of making a mistake.

Teachers with an understanding of child development know that fear is an integral part of growing up. Conceit is an overinflated opinion of one's abilities or sense of self-efficacy. Fear on the other hand is a deep-rooted psychological and physiological reaction to a perceived threat to the self. The reaction can be so intense that it can immobilize a person and at the very least hinder performance. It is presumptuous for teachers to think that they can discount labels that students put on their feelings. The presumption is compounded when teachers change the student's label, especially if the teacher's label is negative.

Informed teachers know that their opinion of students' personal characteristics have a powerful influence on students' self-esteem, self-confidence, and ultimately, on their performance. These teachers exercise extreme caution when making personal statements about students. If a student is fearful or shy about talking in front of a group, I think the teacher should be empathic and try to encourage the student in such a way that the student's feelings are validated but not encouraged. To discourage shyness or fearfulness, teachers can help desensitize shy students by having them practice being before a group as they approx- imate speaking before the group. For example, the shy student can pass papers to the group, can stand in front of the group with other students and participate in a discussion, can be selected to assist the teacher, or call on other students by name. Students should know that some fear is a normal accompaniment of the uncertainty of growing up.

SCENARIO 188:
Damsel in Distress?

I was at lunch in sixth grade and a girl hit me with her purse repeatedly. I chased her down and thumped her in the arm. The lunch monitor took me to the vice-principal and called my mom and said I would have to serve ICS, in-class suspension. My mom took me out of that school and transferred me to private school.

Rx: In this scenario, in which a male student was involved in an altercation with a female student, there are several problems. One problem is a failure to acknowledge that there are two sides to every story and that both sides should be heard. Assuming the lunch monitor was another student leads me to the second problem, the problem of delegating such an important responsibility to children. Piaget (1965) points out in his theory of children's moral reasoning that young children may not consider a person's motive or intent when judging that person's behavior. Another problem is the possibility of gender bias. When a young male and a young female are involved in a conflict, educators and administrators frequently assume that it is the male's fault. Even if a young woman starts a fight and the young man retaliates, he is perceived as picking on a "defenseless" female. A fourth problem is the harshness of the punishment. Males, minority males in particular, tend to receive harsher punishments and more frequent suspensions than females do (Gibbs, 1988).

Fair-minded teachers listen to both sides of the story when there is conflict. These teachers consider the merits of each argument without letting race, gender, or socioeconomic status influence their judgement. If they cannot settle the conflict with verbal reprimands, they make sure that any punishment administered is appropriate and equitable. I do not think a student should be responsible for reporting another student to the vice-principal. A teacher as the lunch monitor may have been able to stop the problem and may never have had to report the incident. Teachers are usually more of a deterrent to misbehavior than student monitors.

SCENARIO 205:
Trust Me at Your Own Risk

My worst experience with a teacher was in high school. I was taking a government class at night and was receiving As on all exams. The last night of class the teacher said we could leave early. When I left the class I had an A. I was apprehended by a school guard on my way out and the teacher was reprimanded for letting me leave. After the guard left, the teacher handed me my grade, which was now a C. When I asked her why my grade had dropped, she accused me of cheating.

Rx: The teacher violated school policy and dismissed her students early. This heedless act spawned a multitude of academic sins. The first sin was possibly jeopardizing the students' safety. Having a guard on the premises suggests a need for precautions. She exhibited displaced anger— anger at the students rather than at the guard or with herself. She did not accept the guard's reprimand gracefully. She did not take responsibility for her actions. She took her anger out on her student who was caught. She lowered that student's grade and finally, she justified the lowered grade by accusing the student of cheating. Unfortunately, her response to being reprimanded undermined her integrity.

Responsible teachers try not to let situations get out of hand, as this one obviously did. The mistake would not have happened if the teacher had observed school policy. Teachers may unintentionally violate policy because they are unaware of school rules, but responsible teachers make it their business to know school policy on important issues. Teachers with integrity take full responsibility for their actions. Good teachers would not let their students suffer any consequences for their own misdeeds. They would not consider lowering a grade or accusing a student of cheating in retaliation for their being reprimanded.

When I was in eighth grade, our home economics teacher let us go home early. We were bussed to the school so we had quite a distance to walk to get home. There was a large group of us, so we stopped at a little candy shop that had a jukebox and we danced and talked and went our separate ways. It was all very innocent but the next day seemed ominous. I had never been in trouble in school before.

The principal came to our room to collect all of the students that left early. The administrators treated us as if we had skipped school. There was talk of suspension, and I was mortified. I do recall looking at my teacher, imploring her to intervene, but she did nothing but look away. I do not think she ever took responsibility for letting us go. She certainly never apologized to us for setting us up for trouble. Fortunately, we were not suspended. I did learn years later that the seemingly innocent "candy shop" was really a front for drug dealers who sold drugs to kids. As I reflect back on my experience, I see the importance of rules and policies that are designed to safeguard children. Teachers should not knowingly violate school policy no matter how well intentioned the situation might be.

SCENARIO 184:
The Whole Is Greater Than Its Parts

Mrs. W. called me up in front of the class to reprimand me for a 68 in spelling on a scholastic achievement test, when I had made a 99 cumulative score overall.

Rx: A classic mistake that teachers and parents make is focusing on the negative and effectively discounting the positive. In this scenario, the teacher virtually ignored the high cumulative score and zeroed in on the low spelling score. The public reprimand was perceived as a punishment. The high cumulative achievement was not recognized or rewarded. This is confusing for the student. It is not clear if the student was a success or a failure at the task.

Savvy teachers know that if they feel they must criticize some aspect of a student's performance, it should certainly be put in proper perspective. In this scenario where the child was weak in spelling but overall did an excellent job, a word of encouragement to improve in spelling and a jubilant focus on the overall accomplishment would be appropriate. Weiner (1979) proposes that we help students to properly attribute their successes and failures to their ability and effort. If a child is confused about their successes and failures, they may never learn to attribute appropriately.

SCENARIO 87:
Excluded!

In my sixth grade drama class after the script was written and handed out to the students, I looked on the character listing and I wasn't even in the script! She had to write me in.

Rx: Sometimes teachers make honest mistakes that can be perceived as having malicious intent. In this scenario, the author obviously believed that the teacher had an ulterior motive in writing her out of the script. Although the teacher wrote her back in, the student was unable to let go of the initial omission. The student apparently internalized the slight, nurtured it, and hung on to it for years. There is no evidence that the teacher was aware of the impact of the omission.

Astute teachers know the importance of apologizing to a student when they make mistakes. I think it is important to preface that apology with an acknowledgement that teachers make honest mistakes and to assure the student that it was not personal. To soothe ruffled feathers, teachers can ask students what else can they do to make them feel better.

SCENARIO 165:
To Err Is Human, to Admit It Is Divine

When I was in sixth grade my English teacher gave me a C on a project. That isn't a bad grade, it could have been worse, but I disagreed with it. The assignment was to make a poster showing the difference between "good" and "well." He said I got the concepts backwards and gave me a C. I was so sure I had them straight. I remember every week in elementary school telling my teacher, "I don't feel good," and she would say, "Well, you don't feel well."

And so I was positive that my picture of a man's face that I put on my poster with a thermometer and sad, droopy, watery eyes saying, "He doesn't feel well" was correct. Wrong, my teacher said. I still believe that I was correct. Even today, I am confused as to how I feel. So I mostly say I have a headache or my stomach hurts. And I seldom correct others on their use of good and well, fearing I might correct them the wrong way and traumatize them for life. I am not really traumatized, but I will never forget all of my hard effort I put into that poster and joy I felt, thinking I finally used the word correctly, only to find out I was wrong and had been misguided.

Rx: This is a scenario of "the student is right and the teacher is wrong." Well can be used as an adjective or adverb to mean in good health, satisfactory, or to appear well dressed; whereas, good is only used as an adjective and it is never used to modify a verb (Warriner & Griffith, 1977). Either the teacher was unaware that he was wrong or reluctant to admit that he was wrong. Erroneously, some teachers believe that because they are the teacher, they must know all of the answers all of the time and never make mistakes. They think that if they admit that they are wrong that their admission is a sign of weakness that undermines their credibility.

The smart, confident teacher realizes that saying "I don't know" and being ignorant for the moment is preferable to never saying "I don't know" and remaining ignorant for all time. When children are so sure they are right, effective teachers give them the opportunity to investigate and tell them that teachers make mistakes and that sometimes the student is right. If the student is right, these teachers readily admit their errors or shortcomings. Teachers can save face and validate the child by thanking the child for the gift of the new knowledge.

SCENARIO 138:
It's Gobbledygook to Me

About the only thing I can remember was my kindergarten teacher. She had an accent but I can't recall where she was from. The problem was that I had trouble understanding her and when she would give directions, I'd do something different. As a result, I'd always get in trouble. This was a daily thing and it got to be a real chore just to go to school. One day, as soon as my mom dropped me off, I ran back home because I was lost with the teacher.

Rx: Clear directions are imperative for student success. The teacher was apparently unaware of her accent and the disorienting effect it had on her oral instructions. Unfortunately, she penalized her students for her unintentional error. It is human nature to be aware of someone else's accent and be oblivious to our own. Unfortunately, she penalized her students for not being able to follow her confusing directions.

Discerning teachers monitor their students' body language, expressions, and tone of voice continuously to detect any signs of miscommunication or misunderstanding. These experienced teachers know the importance of asking the students if the directions are clear. Language or accent may not be a problem, but the difficulty level of the content may make directions confusing. Difficult material should be broken down into manageable chunks and be explained one step at a time. The classroom climate should be warm and friendly enough so students feel free to say they do not understand the directions. Teachers should speak slowly and deliberately and use visuals if possible when they are giving directions. They can demonstrate or model what is to be done. An example and a visual are especially helpful when language is a barrier. If there is still some doubt about the clarity of instructions, teachers can ask other students to explain the directions in their own words or to demonstrate the steps in the directions.

SCENARIO 108:
Your Crime, My Time

I had a Spanish teacher in high school and she had left for maternity leave and she gave me an F because I did not turn in my notebook, but I did. And my mother still put me on restriction. It turned out I got a B.

Rx: If we can assume that the author of the scenario did turn in the notebook assignment, then it is reasonable to assume that the Spanish teacher misplaced or lost the assignment. The teacher's lack of organization became a serious consequence for the student—a failing grade and undeserved punishment. I had a similar incident in my sophomore English class. I turned in a paper and the teacher said I did not turn it in. She wanted me to redo the paper. I was very upset because that meant retyping the paper without the benefit of a correcting typewriter or word processor. I remember telling her that it was our job as students to do the work and turn it in and it was her job to keep up with the work. Coming from a teenager, that was considered an impudent remark. Today, as an adult educator, I would echo that remark with gusto.

Well-organized teachers have routines for collecting assignments, storage of papers, grading, and recording grades. Experienced teachers realize that if they do not have a system and papers are turned in or collected haphazardly or improperly stored, the odds of losing papers increases. If a teacher has lost or misplaced a student's paper, the student should not be penalized in any way. The teacher should take responsibility for the lost paper. If there is even a remote possibility that the student turned in the work, the student should receive the highest possible grade. The rationale is that the student may have earned the highest grade, although that remains an unknown. If it is not too much trouble, teachers can offer students extra credit to resubmit an assignment. When in doubt about whether or not a student turned in an assignment, leave parents out. This avoids providing parents with a reason to punish their children unnecessarily.

6

TEACHING STYLE
AND BEHAVIOR

"Teachers are fighting back against kids who cut class.
Today I was the victim of a drive-by math quiz!"

Mistake
21

Teacher Bias or Expectations

The second semester of my junior year of high school, having been the class clown in Mr. H.'s social studies class, I had determined that I was going to turn over a new leaf with my new teacher. On the first day of class, Mrs. C. immediately announced, "Where is so and so?" I raised my hand and she stated, "I have heard all about you, you need to sit up here!" She then sat me at a desk next to hers. So much for a fresh start.

Rx: Even a class clown deserves a clean slate with a new teacher. The classic study by Rosenthal and Jacobson (1968) suggests that having negative expectations for a student can become a "self-fulfilling prophecy." This action by the teacher was apparently very disheartening for this student who wanted to change. In lieu of a reformed, mature student, this teacher would most likely get a repeat performance of the old disruptive behavior and the student would become a discipline problem as expected. When I was teaching, I intentionally avoided reading any comments about my new students. I preferred to form my own opinions of my students, giving each of them an opportunity to change.

In fact, I had a fifth grade class that I was able to turn around using this strategy. As I recall, there were four teachers on the team. Their policy was to select their classes from the pool of new students. One of the classes did not have an assigned teacher. The team came up with the brilliant idea to place all of the "undesirable" students into the class without a teacher. I was returning from maternity leave and I had the great fortune of inheriting this class. One of the teachers was a close friend of mine. She warned me about my students and apologized for the nightmare class that the teachers had created. I ignored the warning and decided to use the "self-fulfilling prophecy" theory to my advantage. When I met my students for the first time, I was very enthusiastic and excited. I told them how pleased I was to have them as students, because I had heard that I had one of the best classes in the school. I was amused by the way they looked around as if to ask, "Who is she talking to?" This class far exceeded my expectations and certainly those of the other teachers that year.

SCENARIO 173:
Dark Comedy of Gender Bias

In my eighth grade industrial arts class, there were only two girls in the class, including me. The teacher would always take our work and say, "C'mon guys, if a girl can do this good, you guys better at least try to do better than they do." His low expectations because of gender bias could have been devastating, but although irritating, it proved to be humorous too.

Rx: The secret is out. Research findings have shown that teachers' expectations tend to favor males (Block, 1980). This teacher's comments support evidence that traditionally, girls have been expected not to perform as well as boys in predominantly male activities such as industrial arts and sports. When males are not performing up to par they are called "girls" in a very derogatory manner. As this student indicated, these messages are often delivered with humor, but gender bias is dark comedy with lasting effects.

Insightful teachers encourage their students to be more androgynous in their thinking and behavior, meaning that they do not favor masculinity or femininity but respect both. Resourceful teachers use every opportunity to encourage androgyny. They encourage girls to participate in male-dominated activities and boys to embrace more female-oriented activities. Students are always praised for their efforts. These progressive teachers might one day make gender bias an obsolete term.

SCENARIO 250:
Justice for All

My worst experience was staying after school in the first grade. I do not remember the rest of the year. All I know is, my mom had to pick me up from school at least once a week because I had a fever. When I got home I was fine. The fever was gone.

In seventh grade I had a math teacher who was very unfair. If there were a group of us talking in her class, I would get in trouble. When she separated the class I was moved to the very back. She would just treat me more unfairly than the rest of the students.

Rx: Most students are very perceptive about how a teacher feels about them. They keep a watchful eye and constant surveillance of the teacher's actions and reactions, looking for telltale signs of like or dislike. When children conclude that a teacher does not like them, the focus shifts from learning and education to feelings and motives. When a teacher is unfair, children know it.

Master teachers know that fairness is a sterling quality in teachers. Children want their teacher's approval and they deserve to be treated fairly. Caring teachers critique their own behavior frequently to assure themselves that they are not singling out a student for punishment or unfair treatment. Impartial educators insist on fairness for all students, including the ones that they do not like.

SCENARIO 131:
Extraterrestrial Terror

My worst experience in school was no doubt with my kindergarten teacher. She plainly didn't like me and she let everyone know about it every day with her actions.

I think it all started when my mother brought my lunch to school for me. We lived close by, so my mom liked walking over and giving me a nice, warm lunch. My teacher obviously disliked pampered kids, but this was beside the point. She began to treat me more harshly than the other kids. Her voice and tone seemed to be different with me. Every minimal accident on my part, such as spilling paint, called for severe punishment. She constantly threatened to send me to the principal for a paddling. I was always in time-out.

The teacher had an inflatable E.T. that she would place on the table of the quietest student. Knowing that I was deathly afraid of the E.T., she always placed it on my desk, whether I had been quiet or not. I noticed her anger towards me as we filed past her into the room. She patted everyone as they walked past her, but she always skipped me. It got to the point that I refused to go to school. My father took me to school and even though I was crying, she didn't bother to get up and attempt to soothe me. That's when my dad saw her lack of effort.

Rx: The obvious bias described in this scenario is curious. Why would an adult teacher make such

overt gestures of unfair treatment to such a small child? What pathology would motivate such actions? Unfortunately, some unbalanced teachers manage to infiltrate the teaching profession. Many professions are hosts to similar unfortunate souls. In most school districts there are no screening processes in place for new teachers that are sensitive enough to detect deep emotional or mental problems. Maybe the rare instances of getting this type of teacher do not warrant mental screening.

Good teachers are sensitive to a child's need for acceptance and fair treatment. Caring teachers would never do anything to terrorize children, such as constantly showing them a feared object. Caring teachers are always willing to comfort a distressed child, but they wisely regard the legal limitations of their school district. If the district has a hands-off policy, they soothe and comfort with words.

SCENARIO 227:
Liar, Liar, Your Habit's on Fire

I was educated in Catholic school all of my life. With that in mind, I had a bad nun experience. As a young student I was always fearful and intimidated by the older women in their scary black hoods and gowns. This time period would have been in the late sixties when they still wore the full-length battle dress. In my opinion they more closely resembled witches, like the one in the Wizard of Oz, than saintly women who had devoted their lives to the church.

Well, there was this one nun who always had it in for me. No matter where I went or every time I was about to do something she was always there, so I never really had the opportunity. Then one day while in sixth grade, another classmate came running to tell me that my sister, who was a fifth-grader, was in a fight with a boy, so I better get over there, which I did, but there was no sign of a fight, just a mob of kids surrounding my sister and this boy. I quickly got to the center of the mob, as I was about to ask my sister what was going on, I felt some huge force pulling me from behind. When I turned to see who was pulling me toward the outside of the mob, I was surprised to see it was the nun who was always after me. She was grabbing me, saying, "Don't hit that boy anymore." The principal, who was also a nun, then came up and asked what happened and why did this nun have me in a police chokehold. The bad nun then said I was beating up the fifth grader and she had to pull me off of him before I did any more damage. I had no say in this field trial. I was given the mandatory amount of demerits and put on probation, as well as having to do a month of work detail during recess, lunch, and after school. I have never looked at nuns the same after this travesty of justice.

Rx: Are nuns above lying? If we believe this student's account, then clearly they are not. Nuns are people, not saints. They have the same character defects as anyone else. It is certainly plausible that the nun in search of an offense manufactured this story and took advantage of the situation. This "I've-got-my-eye-on-you" behavior is not limited to nuns. Teachers and administrators frequently have this attitude toward problem students. Although some students truly bear watching, for others it is a set-up, a misdeed waiting to happen.

Effective teachers have high standards of integrity and honesty and would never lie about a student. Competent teachers work on helping students to change undesirable behavior. They never perpetuate bad behavior by setting a student up, by falsely accusing a student, or by manufacturing an offense.

SCENARIO 63:
Cheater Watch

My worst experience was in high school when I was a junior. I believe the class was Physical Science and there were about eighteen students in my class. We would go over a couple of chapters and then have an exam. Our teacher gave tough exams—essay type, fill-in-the-blanks. Anyway—not to brag—but I usually got one of the top scores on the exams. This made a few girls angry or jealous, so they told the teacher that I was cheating. Well, I found this out from one of my friends and I confronted the teacher. I told her that I study for the tests and I DO NOT CHEAT. I told her that she could watch me and sit me close to her every time we take a test. Well, she did this—but for some reason I always thought she labeled me as a cheater. I graduated salutatorian of my class, but to this day because of some jealousy and hatred I was labeled a cheater. I did not like the teacher before and I still don't.

Rx: When students decide to blow the whistle on a student for cheating, teachers have an obligation to follow up on the charge. Accusing a student of cheating is a serious offense that invites serious repercussions. It is imperative that teachers consider the motives of the accusers and look out for hidden agendas. The teacher in this scenario took the word of the accusers at face value with no evidence. She communicated her beliefs to the accused student by agreeing to observe that student during the test.

Astute professionals know that high grades are not *prima facie* evidence of cheating. The risks of falsely accusing a child of cheating and of showing an expectation that the child will cheat are great. Accusing a child of cheating is a good way to extinguish the good behavior of making high grades. Students can be expelled for cheating, their reputations can be ruined by rumors of cheating, and they can become disenfranchised by a teacher who thinks they are cheating. Teachers need to tread lightly in the cheating arena, unless they witness the cheating. If a teacher suspects cheating but has no evidence, the best action is no action until there is indisputable proof. In the interim, it is prudent to remind students of the consequences of cheating and to use measures that are incompatible with cheating such as parallel forms of the test. Teachers should never communicate to students that they expect them to cheat or single a child out for strict surveillance. Proximity and movement around the classroom are effective cheating deterrents for most students. Teachers should circulate among students rather than focus attention on one possible cheater. Keep in mind that most students are responsible learners that do not cheat. Trust is a great motivator.

Mistake

22

Unethical Behavior

Scenario 150

There are two incidents that stick out in my mind and they were with the class as a whole and not just me. My sixth grade year I was put in an English class with a bunch of troublemakers. The teacher had a breakdown and quit and the rest of the year the class watched movies and read books out loud.

When I went into my seventh grade class (it was in a different school district), I had a wonderful, but hard, teacher for English, who taught me more than I ever learned before or since.

My second experience was during my senior year of high school. I was taking two English classes with two different teachers, because I was pregnant the previous year. The teacher for my sophomore English class is who I am about to talk about. My sophomore English class was with a bunch of "lower levels" and troublemakers. The teacher told us that none of us would ever go to college. I could not believe this teacher was telling us that. She was a teacher!

Scenario 274

The worst experience I remember having in school was during my senior year in high school. I had just found out I was pregnant with my daughter and had been absent several days from school. I was placed on "homebound" by my doctor. In order to be on homebound I would have to change from my computer course to an elective I could study at home. I went to speak to my computer teacher about dropping the course and she told me, upon finding out I was pregnant, "Why don't you just drop out?" That was the worst thing a student could be told by a teacher.

Rx: In both of these scenarios, the teachers were less than encouraging. They actually discouraged their students by communicating their low expectations for their students. Suggesting that a student drop out of school or that a group of students will never go to college is unethical behavior. Our mission as educators is to try to give every child a good education. We would be appalled if a doctor told a patient, "Why don't you just die, you're probably not going to get any better?" We would think that a doctor's duty is to do everything possible to help the patient get better and to keep the patient alive. The teacher's charge is no less important. The teacher has a duty to help students become better students and to keep hope alive.

Encouraging teachers have high hopes and expectations for their students and communicate their feelings to their students in very loving ways. They make their students work hard and they teach them to believe in themselves. Encouraging teachers help students get enthusiastic about learning and they teach students to persevere. Encouraging teachers seek to inspire students to stay in school and would never suggest that a student drop out, especially a pregnant student. It is imperative that a teenage mother obtains an education. The quality of her baby's future depends on it. Dinkmeyer and Losoncy (1980) offer some strategies for becoming better encouragers in *The Encouragement Book.*

SCENARIO 33:
Out in the Cold

The winter of 1972, the ground was covered with snow. I got in trouble for talking, I think. The teacher told me to get my coat, take a chair, and go stand on the chair in the hallway, which was outside. I stood there the rest of the day, even through lunch. When my sister came to pick me up after school the teacher said I couldn't go. My mother had to come up to the school to get me. Because I was standing in the hallway other classes walked past me on the way to lunch. Other teachers would stop and tell their classes that this is what happens to bad children.

I met this teacher's ex-husband about six years ago (small world). He told me that when she was teaching at that school, she wasn't even certified. When she did get certified, she got kicked out of a school district for having sex with students, went to another school district and did the same thing again. Now she can't teach anywhere, thank God! The teacher did many things that were humiliating and devastating to a child's self-esteem.

Rx: This scenario conjures up an image of a small, bewil-

dered, frozen child, huddled on a chair, informing the masses of her misbehavior by her presence. The teacher obviously wanted to make an example of this child, but she chose a very unethical approach. It is unethical to leave a child outside of the class most of the day for a minor offense. It is particularly offensive to make that child stand outside in cold, freezing weather for a long period of time. Forcing the child to stand out in the cold placed the child at risk for frostbite and other cold-related illnesses. The irony of this intense punishment is that the child was unaware of the offense, which renders the punishment ineffective. The pathology evident in this teacher's behavior underscores the need for better screening of teacher applicants.

Rational teachers are aware that social isolation is more effective if they specify the misbehavior and communicate the desired behavior. Social isolation is not recommended for more than ten minutes. Experienced teachers know that the setting should be somewhat isolated from the class, but the student should be visible at all times. The alone time without reinforcement gives students an opportunity to think. The astute teacher does not use time-out as punishment; instead time-out is an opportunity to regroup and resume appropriate behavior. Qualified, responsible teachers would use tactics that make the punishment fit the crime. They would never put a child in such a risky, inhumane situation.

SCENARIO 127:
Bloody Secret

In the fourth grade I had a female teacher whose name I cannot recall. I do recall that I was acting up on the way out of the room for recess and she grabbed me. She had long red fingernails and when she grabbed me, she dug them deep into my arm. As she did, I jerked my arm and left a considerable amount of flesh under her nails. My arm was bleeding and she wouldn't let me go to the nurse. She just gave me a wet paper towel to put on it and made me sit in the room during the recess period. I never forgot her!

Rx: The overzealous teacher in this scenario accidentally clawed a student with her long, red, and possibly dirty, nails. The scratches were deep enough to draw blood and if the nails were dirty, there was the risk of infection. Injuring the child was terrible, but when the teacher failed to acknowledge that she had hurt the child, that made her offense worse. Denying the child medical attention elevated this offense to unethical status. It seems that the teacher was trying to cover up the incident to avoid any negative repercussions such as a lawsuit or losing her job. Her efforts to protect herself placed her student at risk for infection and further discomfort. She made no effort to comfort the student. She tried to act as if the incident did not happen and she probably secretly hoped that the student would do the same. Then again, maybe she felt that the injury was the child's fault because he pulled away. On the contrary, she was the adult in charge. She inflicted the wound. She was responsible.

The responsible teacher would have apologized to the child immediately and let the child know that she did not mean to hurt him or her. She would take the child to the nurse if possible, acknowledge what happened, and point out that the child pulled away and precipitated the accident. She would make sure the child's injury was attended to and that the child was comfortable before returning to class. If necessary, she would be willing to acknowledge the accident to the class to assure them that the child would be fine. The smart teacher would learn from her mistake and cut her nails or keep her paws off her students as long as she has claws.

SCENARIO 239:
A Lesson in Deception

The worst experience I can remember is plagiarizing my entire senior research paper. My teacher was a man whom I highly respected and thought of as being very scholarly and astute. When he returned my paper, he made a note on it that he could tell it was plagiarized, but still gave me a C and did not make me rewrite it. I learned that sub-average work was acceptable and enough to get by. I also learned that "scholars" could look the other way and lower their standards.

Rx: A high school senior with a developed sense of right and wrong realized that "giving" a student a grade is unethical. Teachers are supposed to model moral and prosocial behaviors. The astute student was quick to detect the dishonesty in the way the teacher graded the paper. He realized that the grade of "C" was not a gift. It was a lesson in deception. The student was obviously disenchanted with the teacher's willingness to look the other way. It suggested that the teacher had low expectations for the student. The teacher's motive could have been to seek the approval of his students. Perhaps he was giving the student the benefit of a doubt. Whatever the motive, the action was inappropriate.

The best "gift" a teacher can give a student is honest feedback that will help to improve the student's performance. Expecting students to do the right thing is an added bonus. Discerning teachers are unwilling to accept anything less than a student's personal best. If they suspect that they are getting less, they send students back to the drawing board for a redo. These caring actions teach children to strive for excellence and to take "good enough" out of their performance vocabulary. Most of all, wise teachers make their students accountable. Plagiarism carries heavy consequences. Students who knowingly plagiarize should have consequences that are not rewarding. Good teachers only give students grades that they earn, no more and no less.

SCENARIO 209:
Sneaky Snacking

In sixth grade a friend and I made cupcakes for our third period class. The teacher accused C. and me of each stealing one cupcake. Two were missing. Well, she accused us in class and we told her we didn't do it. I then proceeded to tell her that she probably ate them. I was sent to the office but I stopped by my uncle's room (he was a teacher at the school), told him what happened, and we both went to the principal. We went back to the teacher's room and found the wrappers in the trashcan under her desk.

Rx: Teachers are not immune to the frailties of man. The teacher's behavior in this scenario appears to have been deliberate unethical behavior on the surface, but closer inspection suggests an eating disorder. People who steal food, sneak and eat it, then lie about it may have an eating disorder. If the food substance is a carbohydrate, that is usually a telling sign. Sometimes people with eating disorders eat compulsively and need food, much like an addict that needs a drug. This eating disorder is often known as food addiction. Food is the food addict's "drug" and like other addicts, they will do whatever they can to get their substance, even lie about little sixth-grade children.

I often caution my pre-service teachers to empty their emotional baggage before they enter the teaching profession. Claudia Black (1991) and other researchers have found that children from alcoholic households usually develop addictions themselves and flock to "helping" professions as adults. Teaching is a helping profession that attracts adult children of alcoholics (ACOAs). There is a body of literature available on the subject of ACOAs. I recommend that pre-service teachers from alcoholic homes read this literature and visit the ACOA support groups where they can learn to break the cycle of addiction and counter its ill effects. Prudent teachers recognize the value of working on their issues before they enter the classroom. Awareness and action would make situations like lying about students and stealing food unnecessary and nonexistent. Wise teachers know that they destroy their credibility if they lie to or about their students. It is critical to the learning process that students perceive their teachers as trustworthy. The quality of teacher-pupil relationships affects how students learn (Flanders & Morine, 1973).

SCENARIO 220:
Teacher Goes AWOL

My bad teacher experience occurred when I was in the ninth grade and we had a big earthquake (1987). During the earthquake my teacher decided to run out of the room. The students were scared to death, yet no one spoke. We stayed inside the classroom until the evacuation team came to inspect the room. They were shocked to find us still inside. About fifteen minutes had passed. We never saw our teacher again.

Rx: The most difficult aspect of a crisis is the critical period of indecision that usually triggers the fight or flight response. The teacher in this scenario made the inappropriate choice of running away from the crisis and abandoning her students. As a result, her students were not evacuated immediately. This teacher's actions could have put her students' lives in jeopardy.

Skilled teachers know that in a crisis situation flight is not an option, especially when children are involved. The nature of the relationship of teachers and students places the teachers in *loco parentis* (in the position of the parent) as dictated by common law (Reutter, 1975). Competent professionals recognize the serious nature of their charge and act reasonably to protect the welfare and best interests of the children. Sometimes the call of duty dictates that teachers place their students' best interests before their own. In this scenario, the teacher had a responsibility to stay with the students and make sure that they were evacuated safely. Parents have a right to assume that schools will do everything in their power to protect their children. Most teachers are good, dedicated people who would do whatever is necessary to protect their students. In the 1999 Littleton, Colorado, shooting crisis (Shore, 1999), a teacher sacrificed his life for his students. The teacher in this scenario was not prepared for this aspect of teaching—that's probably why she was never seen again.

Mistake
23

False Accusations

My vocational drafting teacher accused me of not doing my own work because years prior to my being in his class two of my brothers had him as their teacher. He thought all of my projects had been done by them.

Rx: Current research suggests that schools shortchange girls in many ways (AAUW, 1992). The male teacher in this scenario provided evidence of one of those ways. He refused to give his female student credit for her work. His obvious gender bias prevented an objective appraisal of his student's work. He thought that her work had been done by her brothers. It seems that he was acting under the influence of gender stereotypes rather than accusing her of cheating. Whatever his motive, his behavior was clearly a strike against the equal treatment of males and females. It is less probable that he would tell a young male that a female did his work for him. Failure to give female students credit where credit is due diminishes the self-esteem and motivation of female students.

Progressive male teachers are aware of the negative effects of gender bias. They seek to promote the accomplishments of both male and female students. They try not to promote sexual stereotyping. Instead, they encourage students to assume nontraditional roles and expect them to do well in those roles. These teachers would not go so far as to accuse a student of having someone else do her work simply because the teacher's views are firmly entrenched in gender stereotypes.

SCENARIOS 30, 38, 112, & 128:
Arbitrary Scapegoats

Scenario 30

It was in sixth grade, we were working on an art project and someone lost the project. The teacher (Sister A. we called her sister Asusta—it means scary), accused me of stealing it and basically humiliated me in front of the class. I started crying and kept on telling her that I had not taken the vase. We were making a paper-maché vase. The vase turned up from someone else. She never apologized to me about what she had said.

Scenario 38

In orchestra we had to perform our tests, sometimes live, this time on tape. The next day, the teacher was angry because the tape machine was used incorrectly. She blamed me and reprimanded me in front of the class as the one who messed it up. It wasn't me. J.W. did it and he admitted it later. I was made to feel embarrassed in front of everyone when I wasn't at fault. She never apologized to me privately or publicly.

Scenario 112

I was in kindergarten when I was accused of throwing rocks on the playground. I had to sit down the rest of recess. My teacher went on the word of her pet student. I was not a troublemaker in class so I was really upset. I remember that I just sat there and cried.

Scenario 128

The teacher that I least like to remember is Ms. M. She was my sixth grade homeroom teacher. I really didn't like her because it seemed that she was always in a bad mood. She seemed to always take it out on us. She would never let us go to the restroom. Well, I guess the real reason that I didn't like her is because she wanted to punish me for something I didn't do. This girl who sat next to me, M., was throwing staples across the room. One accidentally hit Ms. M. on the neck. She asked the students who it was and they said it came from the direction that I was sitting in. So I was accused of this. I kept telling her that it wasn't me. Even M. denied it and said it was me, but it wasn't. So, I was sent to the office. My mom was called and I told her what happened. My mom believed me, but the vice-principal didn't. The only reason they didn't punish me is because my mom swore she wouldn't let the issue rest. After that I didn't like Ms. M. much.

Rx: The students in these scenarios were all impulsively selected to bear the blame for someone else's misdeeds. None of the teachers actually saw the accused student do anything wrong. They would each have to examine their consciences or biases to determine why they arbitrarily selected the students they accused. Teachers who make accusations without any evidence or proof have a number of reasons for justifying their accusatory actions: the student looks sneaky, guilty, nervous, or suspicious; they don't like the student; or maybe they don't trust the student. In some of these cases, students are guilty by association or by proximity.

When these teachers feel personally touched by a wrongdoing, they look for someone to blame. When there is doubt, they will settle for a scapegoat.

Prudent teachers only make accusations when there is unquestionable proof. They usually rely on what they see and hear, but they are aware that sometimes they can be mistaken. These teachers tread lightly when there is uncertainty. They avoid making oral or written statements about a student that they can't prove because they could be sued for libel or slander. In Scenario 30, a teacher accused the student of stealing a vase. She made the accusation in front of a third party, the class. Froyen (1993) contends that the teacher's comments could be construed as slanderous if they subjected the student to the scorn of a third party, namely the class. Teachers can also be sued if they spread this information and damage a student's reputation. Good teachers are hypervigilant about what they say about students in the presence of the class.

Mistake

24

Inappropriate Reactions

My worst experience was with my fifth grade teacher, Ms. F. I remember it was my first oral report and everyone, including myself, was terrified. We had been working for quite some time on the assignment: learning all about library research, how to set up a presentation, etc. She asked for volunteers and one student presented. Then, she asked for volunteers again and no one raised their hand. I will never forget how that woman flipped out! She started yelling and told us all we were cowards and everyone would be receiving an F. I lost all respect for that teacher. Everyone had worked so hard. She offered no encouragement for us and didn't give us the opportunity for success.

Rx: An important principle of classroom management is that teachers should provide an environment that is conducive to learning. An important principle of assessment is that teachers should provide meaningful, relevant feedback. An important principle of behavior modification is to use praise rather than punishment and humiliation because studies show that praise and encouragement are more effective. An important principle of motivation is to give students an opportunity to experience success, to promote future success. The teacher in this scenario violated all of the above principles. She provided a puni-tive environment that was not conducive to learning. She threatened to give everyone an F, which was meaningless, false feedback. She punished her students by yelling at them, calling them names, and giving them a bad grade. She effectively denied the students an opportunity for success by ignoring their hard work.

Knowledgeable teachers are very cognizant of these principles and employ them at every opportunity. They would know that something was amiss if all of the students were reluctant to volunteer. Perhaps the students needed practice or needed to be desensitized to speaking before a group of people because it was their first time giving an oral report. Wise teachers would take into consideration that fifth grade heralds the onset of puberty for many students, which adds a new variable to the shyness equation. Sensible teachers would recognize the futility of punishing students for their reluctance and would know the consequences of denying the students an opportunity for success. They know that they would extinguish the good, productive behavior of their students by failing to recognize their hard work and effort. The teacher in this scenario should have resisted an angry, ineffective outburst and exercised patience, understanding, praise, and practice to achieve desirable outcomes.

SCENARIO 40:
Silence Is Not Always Golden

When I was in second or third grade I experienced a very embarrassing moment that I have never forgotten. My class was in the lunchroom with all of the other classes. Because the noise level had reached a high level, the principal, who monitored the lunchroom daily, had called a "silent lunch." This meant that no one in the lunchroom was supposed to be talking, for any reason.

For about twenty-five minutes the room had been quiet, and my class was about to be dismissed. As I packed the remains of my lunch back in my lunchbox, I dropped a napkin and whispered to the person next to me, asking them to pick it up. At this moment the principal came up behind me and screamed, "Young lady, do you know what silent lunch means? I suggest you shut your mouth." I was very hurt and embarrassed and have never forgotten that experience.

Rx: The concept of a "silent" lunch as a punishment for talking is a throwback to the tactics used in character education or moral education that was popular during the late nineteenth and early twentieth centuries (Sprinthall et al., 1994). The assumption was that children learn best when everything is quiet. "Good" teachers with "good" control had the quietest classrooms. This obsolete approach presumed that teachers had an obligation to keep students quiet. There was no flexibility and zero tolerance for noncompliance. This obsolete practice of "no talking and I mean no talking" still contaminates many classrooms today.

Informed teachers have abandoned the penal model of education where children are treated as if they are in jail. They realize that they cannot teach children to be independent, self-directing, and responsible by insisting that they be docile, dependent, and controlled by teachers (Sprinthall et al., 1994). Sensitive teachers recognize that children are humans, not pawns. It is human to want to communicate and enjoy other people. It is inhumane to demand silence from children all day. Most adults would balk at such treatment. Flexible teachers would never insist on absolute silence and certainly would not embarrass or humiliate a child for such a minor breach as whispering. Recess and lunch periods should belong to the children; it is their free time. Teachers and administrators should respect that.

SCENARIO 8:
Abandoning the Band

The worst experience that I can remember from my high school years took place when I was drum major of the high school marching band and I was conducting a practice on the football field during class time. In the middle of practice, the band instructor threw up his hands and left the field for the rest of the period. I was left to fend for myself in front of the entire band. Although I was used to doing this, I had never had to conduct the band when the disagreement between the director (the real person with authority) and myself had been so blatantly obvious. It was really hard for me to retain my authority among my peers when the person who was supposed to be backing my authority had abandoned ship, so to speak.

In this particular situation, I felt that the instructor handled things in a really unprofessional manner. As a kid, I felt confused and wondered what I had done that was so wrong. In retrospect, I feel that the instructor (as the adult in charge) should have controlled his emotions and dealt with the problem in a more reasonable and adult-like manner.

Rx: The band director who threw up his hands and left the field seemed to be very frustrated and stressed. One explanation for his abandonment of his students may be *selective avoidance* (Charles, 1983). Selective avoidance is when a person who is highly stressed simply avoids anything and anybody that causes stress.

A professional educator knows that leaving a source of stress may be appropriate for some situations, but it's not always prudent or advisable. Although the drum major is frequently in charge of the band, the teacher is ultimately responsible for the class, not the student. He should have stayed unless there were other adults present. Most teachers realize that delegating students to help with some of the tasks of teaching can reduce stress. Effective delegation is good; shifting responsibility is not. Wise teachers know that it is unwise to leave a class, including a band, unattended with a student in charge. There are unpleasant legal consequences if something goes wrong and the teacher was not there to assure that every effort was made to prevent the occurrence. As the student suggested, the band director should have faced the music in a more adult-like manner by telling the student what was wrong and by working with the student for a solution.

SCENARIO 80:
Oops! Too Bad for You

One day another student knocked over my desk. The teacher watched and snickered. I had to pick up my desk myself and tried not to cry. There were no apologies from teacher or student. It was difficult to concentrate the rest of the day. I thought I had done something wrong.

Rx: Every person has a radius of personal space that encompasses their person and their belongings. When an outsider trespasses in their personal space, the person is entitled to an apology. This is in accordance with the conventions of our society. Failure to give an apology or show contrition is considered bad manners or rude behavior. It also sends a silent message that the person who is violated is not valued. When teachers condone rude behavior and fail to demand an apology for bad behavior, they rubber-stamp the lack of value for this person. Teachers who laugh at a student's misfortune communicate that they do not care about that student.

Effective teachers are aware of the obligation to model and expect good behavior. In this scenario, the teacher should have demanded an apology for the student whose desk was knocked over. Insightful teachers would realize the importance of making the child who knocked over the desk go back and pick the desk up and put it back. Teachers have a professional duty to suppress any bias they might feel and to insist on fair, courteous treatment of all students.

SCENARIO 134:
The Smoke Detector

My worst experience with a teacher was in fourth grade with Mrs. D., I swear this lady hated me. I was home sick for three days, maybe a week, so I had a lot of take-home work to complete. Back then my mom smoked, and my papers must have stunk with cigarette smoke. Well the day I got back to school, I went up to the teacher's desk to turn in my papers. I don't know if it was one of her bad days or not, but she goes and just throws my papers on the floor. I was so embarrassed. I wanted to cry. The class got real silent. No one liked what she did. She told me to pick up my papers and put them on the windowsill to air out. This happened before lunch, and at lunch everyone in my class was sympathetic.

When I got home I told my mom about the incident and she called Mrs. D., who said that she was allergic to cigarette smoke and that was why she did what she did and she said she was sorry. However, I think she could have handled the situation better. The reason I don't believe she liked me was because throughout that year she would do or act in such a way that you knew she didn't like you. I could feel it. A few years later I came across her again when she was a judge for a science contest. Her attitude let me know that she didn't like me.

Rx: Children are very insightful. They also are very sensitive to whether a teacher likes them or not. In this scenario, it is apparent that the teacher did not care too much for this student. It is conceivable that the teacher might have an impulsive knee-jerk reaction to cigarette smoke, but this reaction should have been tempered by concern for the student's feelings. Her cold, callused reaction of having the student pick up the papers she threw down screamed out her disdain for this poor student. She did not bother to explain her actions to the student, which clearly revealed her contempt. The teacher managed to indulge her scorn for this student at a tremendous cost. She lost the respect of her class and she undermined her credibility as a good teacher.

Caring teachers exercise tact in dealing with troublesome situations that have the potential to harm or humiliate students. In the process of trying to resolve the problem, they are sensitive to the child's feelings and seek to speak and act in ways that are not offensive. Sensitive teachers would not say anything to the child because the smoke was not the child's fault. Instead, they would find an inconspicuous way to air out the papers, preferably not in the child's presence.

SCENARIO 179:
What's My Name?

My seventh grade science teacher was absent for the day so we had a substitute. When it was time to call roll she mispronounced my name. I corrected her in a nice manner and she told me to either say here or present and then she told me not to correct her. She said my name wrong again so I corrected her again. Then she moved me to the back, wrote me up and sent me to the principal's office. The principal was busy, but the next day my science teacher apologized and I did not get in trouble.

Rx: This scenario appears very innocent and straightforward on the surface. Important variables here are the student's tone of voice and intent. Was the student being rude? Was the second correction an attempt to test the limit? Was it an innocent attempt to get the teacher to pronounce the name correctly? The answers to those questions are not apparent. What is apparent is that regardless of the student's motive or intent, the teacher overreacted and imposed some stiff penalties as a consequence.

Experienced teachers know that student rudeness appears in a variety of forms: tone of voice, body language, pitch and inflection of voice, backtalk, defiance, and so on. A default reaction to rudeness is anger, aggression, punitive behavior, and so on. However, competent teachers manage to handle rude responses in a professional manner, suppressing any urges to lash out. In this scenario, the teacher could have avoided the power struggle over the name by apologizing and by making a concerted effort to pronounce the name correctly. If the name is too difficult, the teacher could promise to work on getting it right. Students have a right to expect that their teachers will attach enough value to them as a person to pronounce their name correctly.

SCENARIO 189:
Copycat?

One of the most humiliating moments in high school was when my senior year English teacher accused me of plagiarizing. I had spent several days working very hard on a research paper. When I received the paper a week later I was surprised because I had received a C on the paper. I spoke with the teacher about my grade. He told me that he thought I had copied an article or some sort of publication. The fact of the matter is that I used vocabulary in the paper that I was not accustomed to writing and since I took an effort to increase my vocabulary skills I was punished. I felt humiliated.

Rx: Behavioral Learning Theory (Skinner, 1950) makes it clear that in operant conditioning an organism will not persist in a behavior if reinforcement is withheld. In this scenario, an appropriate grade is the reinforcer. The teacher apparently had low expectations for the student and effectively penalized the student for improvement. He gave the student an inappropriate grade of C, as punishment for what he believed was plagiarism. Getting a lowered grade for improved performance could extinguish efforts to improve performance in the future.

Wise teachers are not willing to jeopardize student improvement by failing to give credit where credit is due. They would prefer to err on the side of giving too much credit rather than not enough. This is especially true when there is not enough evidence to warrant the latter. A teacher should only accuse a student of plagiarism when there is indisputable proof.

Mistake

25

Sexual Harassment

SCENARIO 300:
Scratch My Back, I'll Scratch Yours

The worst encounter I had with a teacher was when I joined Number Sense, a UIL competition, and I was hit on by my algebra teacher. I felt that if I didn't comply I would not pass the class. I hated to go to my algebra class because he always called on me and never acknowledged the other girls. I was always teased and everyone would always ask me where's my boyfriend, the algebra teacher, Mr. C. I hated my sophomore year in H.S. because of this. What made matters worse was that on Fridays as a cheerleader I had to wear my uniform with my little skirt and that made me feel very uncomfortable!

Rx: Teachers like this teacher clearly violate sexual harassment laws. Sexual harassment is not limited to unwanted sexual advances. It includes words or acts that demean a person on the basis of sex. The Equal Employment Opportunity Commission recognizes two types of sexual harassment that can conceptually be used in claims of harassment. "Quid pro quo," or something for something, occurs when a superior seeks sex in exchange for a decision. In this scenario, the teacher is the superior and the quid pro quo is the course grade. A second type of harassment is "hostile environment," where unwelcome sexual advances create an offensive environment (Huston, 1993).

The student said she was uncomfortable with the teasing of other students, wearing short skirts around the teacher, and his overly attentive response to her in class. Title IX of the Education Amendments of 1972 guarantees students protection from sexual harassment in schools (Crumpler, 1993). New legislation that holds schools liable for sexual harassment will trigger a more aggressive response to these types of claims. Schools will not want to invite lawsuits. A new ruling allows sexually harassed students to collect monetary damages from schools and school officials if they know of the harassment and ignore it. Schools have to show that they took some action and tried to alleviate the situation. An easy, acceptable action would be to suspend or fire the offending employee. This teacher is not just flirting with a child; he's flirting with disaster. He may end up in a full-blown love affair with disgrace and dismissal. True professionals would never misuse their position to take advantage of vulnerable students. Teachers have a duty to report any sexual harassment that is reported to them.

SCENARIO 100:
Let the Student Beware

I was sitting in band class in the front row when a boy came up behind me and sprayed my butt with a water gun. I had on light-colored pants with blue polka-dot underwear. I was a freshman and he was a junior.

Rx: The male student in this scenario sprayed a female student with a water gun. It seems like an innocent prank but the sexual overtones of his act puts him, his school, and school officials in danger of sexual harassment charges. Unfortunately, playing around will not be an adequate defense. Schools will no longer turn a blind eye or deaf ear to claims of sexual harassment; they will act swiftly and assertively if they are made aware of it.

Competent teachers will be aware of the new ruling that protects students from sexual harassment under Title IX. These teachers will make sure their students are aware of the dos and don'ts of interacting with other students. Teachers may use role-playing to help students understand which behaviors step over the line into sexual harassment territory. It is imperative that students are taught that they can no longer tease or ridicule or touch or engage in unwanted sexual conduct with other students.

SCENARIO 25:
Biting Remarks Beget Big Bucks

I was in geometry my sophomore year in high school. I sat around several guys and yes, we did talk a lot. This one particular day my pencil fell off my desk and landed under one of the guy's desks. I asked him to get it for me. Well, guess who heard us talking? I tried to explain that my pencil had fallen under his desk and she said, "Why didn't you just get it?" I said, "Well, because it's under his legs." Then she made the comment, "I'm sure you've been there before." I did discuss this with the vice-principals because I was an aide for them. Of course, nothing came of it, it just blew over.

Rx: This teacher made a lewd, sexually suggestive comment that could cause her to lose her job in today's environment. The new Supreme Court ruling would hold the school liable because they ignored the student's complaint and did nothing. They might bring themselves into compliance if they established policies that prohibit any form of harassment.

Competent teachers would encourage students to come forward without retaliation or repercussions. These teachers should actively investigate and try to remedy the situation immediately.

Skilled teachers would offer conferences with students in a confidential manner that preserves their anonymity. However, no school personnel would be encouraged to take corrective action without previous investigation. These suggestions are adaptations of EEOC guidelines (Huston, 1993). The teacher's remarks and the school's indifference toward them could cost the school a great deal of money if they are sued. Schools and teachers must become hypervigilant in their efforts to combat harassment in any form.

SCENARIO 235:
Bottoms Up

The classroom was long and narrow with long tables pushed together down the middle. The students sat in a row on either side of the tables. I guess I was up on the chair with one foot, to reach something on the other side. Leaning over a table, the teacher slapped me on the bottom. I had a dress on. I guess my panties were showing. I was embarrassed and humiliated, and it is the only thing I remember from first grade, except that I learned to read from a book about Dick and Jane and Spot. I don't remember having any other interactions with the teacher.

Rx: It is not clear if the teacher in this scenario is a man or a woman. It really does not matter because sexual harassment laws do not discriminate, males and females are equally liable. Slapping a child on the bottom can be construed as a form of sexual harassment. It was probably an impulsive act, but because the slap was on the little girl's somewhat exposed backside, the slap could be perceived as having sexual connotations. Astute teachers know that touching students on the private parts of

their bodies is taboo, forbidden, prohibited, and any other word that conveys the serious nature of this offense. Smart teachers know that the cost of such an act can be prohibitive in terms of financial and professional capital. These teachers are not willing to sacrifice their careers or the school's budget to indulge an impulsive act of impropriety. Knowledgeable teachers would have simply told the student to sit down and that would have solved the problem.

References

American Association of University Women. (1992). *How schools short change girls*. Washington, DC: Author.

American Heritage Dictionary of the English Language (3rd ed.). (1992). Houghton Mifflin. Electronic version licensed from InfoSoft International, Inc. All rights reserved.

Anderson, L. M. (1989). Learners and learning. In M. Reynolds (Ed.), *Knowledge base for beginning teachers* (pp. 85-100). New York: Pergamon.

Bandura, A. (1986). *Social foundations of thought and action: A social cognitive theory*. Englewood Cliffs, NJ: Prentice Hall.

Banks, J., & Banks, C. A. M. (1993). *Multicultural education: Issues and perspectives* (2nd ed.). Boston: Allyn & Bacon.

Belenky, M. F., Clinchy, B. M., Goldberger, N. R., & Tarule, J. M. (1986). *Women's ways of knowing: The development of self, voice, & mind*. New York: Basic Books.

Black, C. (1991). *It will never happen to me*. New York: Ballantine.

Block, J. H. (1980). Promoting excellence through mastery learning. *Theory Into Practice, 19*(1), 66-74.

Bradshaw, J. (1988). *Healing the shame that binds you*. Dearfield Beach, FL: Health Communications.

Brophy, J. (1982). Research on teacher effects: Uses and abuses. *Elementary School Journal, 89*(1), 3-21.

Brophy, J., & Evertson, C. M. (1981). *Student characteristics and teaching*. New York: Longman.

Campbell, L., Campbell, B., & Dickinson, D. (1996). *Teaching and learning through multiple intelligences* (p. 282). Needham Heights, MA: Allyn & Bacon.

Canfield, J. (1990). Improving student's self-esteem. *Educational Leadership, 48*(1), 48-50.

Canter, L., & Canter, M. (1992). *Assertive discipline: Positive behavior management for today's classroom*. Santa Monica, CA: Lee Canter & Associates.

Charles, C. M. (1983). *A handbook of excellence in teaching: Elementary classroom management*. New York: Longman.

Clifford, M. M. (1990). Students need challenge, not easy success. *Educational Leadership, 48*(1), 22-26.

Collier, V. P. (1992). The Canadian bilingual immersion debate: A synthesis of research findings. *Studies in Second Language Acquisition, 14*, 87-97.

Concise Columbia Encyclopedia. (1995). New York: Columbia University Press.

Crumpler, L. E. (1993). Sexual harassment in schools. *NASB Employee Relations Quarterly, 1(4),* 5.

Cuban, L. (1984). *How teachers taught: Constancy and change in American classrooms 1890-1980.* New York: Longman.

Cushner, K., McCelland, A., & Safford, P. (1992). *Human diversity in education: An integrative approach.* St. Louis, MO: McGraw-Hill.

DeCecco, J., & Richards, A. (1974). *Growing pains: Uses of school conflicts.* New York: Aberden.

deCharms, R. (1976). *Enhancing motivation.* New York: Irvington.

Delgado-Gaitan, C. (1990). *Literacy for empowerment: The role of parents in children's education.* New York: Falmer.

Delpit, L. (1988). The silenced dialogue: Power and pedagogy in educating other people's children. *Harvard Educational Review, 58(3),* 280-298.

DeMott, R. M. (1982). Visual Impairments. In N. Haring (Ed.), *Exceptional children and youth* (pp. 271-295). Columbus, OH: Merrill.

Dinkmeyer, D., & Losoncy, L. E. (1980). *The encouragement book: Becoming a positive person.* Englewood Cliffs, NJ: Prentice Hall.

Dreikurs, R. B., Grunwald, B. B., & Pepper, F. C. (1982). *Maintaining sanity in the classroom: Classroom management techniques* (2nd ed.). New York: Harper & Row.

Education of All Handicapped Children Act, Public Law 94-142. (1975). *Individuals with Disabilities Education Act (IDEA).* Last amended 1990 (P.L. 101-476).

Eisenberg, N., & Harris, J. D. (1984). Social competence: A developmental perspective. *The School Psychology Review, 13(3),* 267-277.

Elkind, D. (1989). Developmentally appropriate education for 4-year-olds. *Theory Into Practice, 28(1),* 47-52.

Epanchin, B. C., Townsend, B., & Stoddard, K. (1994). *Constructive classroom management: Strategies for creating positive learning environments.* Pacific Grove, CA: Brooks/Cole.

Erikson, E. (1963). *Childhood and society* (2nd ed.). New York: Norton.

Flanders, N. A., & Morine, G. (1973). The assessment of proper control and suitable learning environment. In N. L. Gage (Ed.), *Mandated evaluation of educators: A conference on California's Stull Act.* Stanford: California Center for Research and Development in Teaching.

Froyen, L. A (1993). *Classroom management: The reflective teacher-leader* (2nd ed.). New York: Macmillan.

Gagne, R. (1977). *Conditions of learning* (3rd ed.). New York: Holt, Rinehart & Winston.

Galloway, C. (1977). Nonverbal. *Theory Into Practice, 16(3),* 129-133.

Garcia, E. E. (1995). Educating Mexican American students: Past treatment and recent developments in theory, research, policy, and practice. In J. A. Banks & C. A. M. Banks (Eds.), *Handbook of research on multicultural education* (pp. 372-381). New York: Macmillan.

Gardner, H. (1993). *Multiple intelligences: The theory in practice.* New York: Basic Books.

Gearheart, B. R., Weishahn, M. W., & Gearheart, C. W. (1992). *The exceptional child in the regular classroom* (5th ed.). Upper Saddle River, NJ: Merrill/Prentice Hall.

Gelman, D. (1983, November 7). A great emptiness. *Newsweek, 102*(1), 120-126.

Gersten, R. (1996). Literacy instruction for minority students: The transition years. *The Elementary School Journal, 96,* 227-244.

Gibbs, J. (1988). *Young, black, and male in America: An endangered species.* Dover, MA: Auburn House.

Glaser, R., & Silver, E. (1994). *Assessment, testing and instruction.* Pittsburgh, PA: Learning Research and Development Center.

Good, T. L., & Brophy, J. E. (1991). *Looking in classrooms* (5th ed.). New York: HarperCollins.

Good, T. L., & Brophy, J. E. (1994). *Looking in classrooms* (6th ed.). New York: HarperCollins.

Good, T. L., & Brophy, J. E. (1997). *Looking in classrooms* (7th ed.). New York: Longman.

Gottfredson, G. D. (1984). *How schools and families can reduce youth crime.* Baltimore, MD: Center for Social Organization of Schools, Johns Hopkins University.

Gronlund, N. E. (1995). *How to write and use instructional objectives.* Upper Saddle River, NJ: Merrill/Prentice Hall.

Harvard University. (1988). Student questions in K-12 classrooms. *Harvard Education Letter,* (1), 7.

Heath, S. (1983). *Ways with words: Language, life, and work in communities and classrooms.* Cambridge MA: Cambridge University Press.

Henson, D. T., & Eller, B. F. (1999). *Educational psychology for effective teaching.* Belmont, CA: Wadsworth.

Huston, T. C. (1993). Handling sexual harassment complaints. *NASB Employee Relations Quarterly, 1*(2), 6.

Irving, O., & Martin, J. (1982). Withitness: The confusing variable. *American Educational Research Journal, 19,* 313-319.

Johnson, D. W., Johnson, R., Dudley, B., Ward, M., & Magnuson, D. (1995). The impact of peer mediation training on the management of school and home conflicts. *American Educational Research Journal, 32*(4), 829-844.

Kauffman, J. M. (1989). *Characteristics of behavioral disorders of children and youth* (4th ed.). Columbia, OH: Merrill.

Kerman, S., & Martin, M. (1980). *Teacher expectations and student achievement: Teacher handbook.* Bloomington, IN: Phi Delta Kappa.

Kindsvatter, R., Wilen, W., & Ishler, M. (1988). *Dynamics of effective teaching.* New York: Longman.

Lancon, J. A., Haines, D. E., & Parent, A. D. (1998). Anatomy of the shaken baby syndrome. *Anatomical Record (New Anatomy), 253,* 13-18.

Levin, J., & Nolan, J. F. (1996). *Principles of classroom management: A professional decision-making model.* Boston: Allyn & Bacon.

Lindholm, K. J., & Fairchild, H. H. (1990). Evaluation of an elementary school bilingual immersion program. In A. M. Padilla, H. H. Fairchild, & C. M. Valdez (Eds.), *Bilingual education: Issues and strategies* (pp. 91-105). Newbury Park, CA: Sage.

MacDonald, R. E. (1991). *A handbook of basic skills and strategies for beginning teachers.* New York: Longman.

Macias, R. (1986). *Teacher preparation for bilingual education.* Report of the Compendium of Papers on the Topic of Bilingual Education of the Committee on Education and Labor House of Representatives, 99th Congress, 2D Session. Washington, DC: U.S. Government Printing Office, 1986, pp. 43-44.

Maple, S. A., & Stage, F. K. (1991). Influences on the choice of math/science major by gender and ethnicity. *American Educational Research Journal, 28*(1), 37-60.

Maslow, A. H. (1970). *Motivation and personality.* New York: Harper & Row.

Mason, D. A., & Good, T. L. (1993). Effects of two-group and whole-class teaching on regrouped elementary students' mathematics achievement. *American Educational Research Journal, 30,* 328-360.

McConnell, S. R., & Odom, S. L. (1986). Sociometrics: Peer referenced measures and the assessment of social competence. In P. S. Strain, M. J. Gralnick, & H. M. Walker (Eds.), *Children's social behavior: Development, assessment, and modification.* Orlando, FL: Academic Press.

McFee, I. N. (1918). *The teacher, the school, and the community.* New York: American.

Messick, S. (1984). The nature of cognitive styles: Problems and promise in educational practice. *Educational Psychologist, 19,* 59-74.

Moll, L. C., & Diaz, S. (1985). Ethnographic pedagogy: Promoting effective bilingual instruction. In E. E. Garcia & R. V. Padilla (Eds.), *Advances in bilingual education research* (pp. 127-149). Tucson: University of Arizona Press.

O'Connor, M. (1998). The power of feedback: Improving standards by identifying children's need via assessment. *Times Educational Supplement, 4258,* 22.

O'Leary, K. D., Kaufman, K. F., Kass, R. E., & Drabman, R. E. (1970). The effects of loud and soft reprimands on the behavior of disruptive students. *Exceptional Children, 37,* 145-155.

O'Leary, K. D., & O'Leary, S. G. (1972). *Classroom management: The successful use of behavior modification* (p. 152). New York: Pergammon.

Orange, C. (1997). Gifted students and perfectionism. *Roeper Review, 20*(1), 39-41.

Orange, C. (in press). Using peer models to teach self-regulation. *The Journal of Experimental Education.*

Ormrod, J. E. (1998). *Educational psychology: Developing learners* (2nd ed.). Englewood Cliffs, NJ: Prentice Hall.

Piaget, J. (1952). *The language and thought of the child.* London: Routledge & Kegan Paul.

Piaget, J. (1965). *The moral judgment of the child.* New York: Free Press.

Renzulli, J. S., & Reis, S. M. (1991). The schoolwide enrichment model: A comprehensive plan for the development of creative productivity. In N. Colangelo & G. Davis (Eds.), *Handbook of gifted education* (pp. 111-141). Boston: Allyn & Bacon.

Reutter, E. (1975). *The courts and student conduct.* Topeka, KS: National Organization on Legal Problems of Education.

Rogers, C. R. (1969). *Freedom to learn.* Columbus, OH: Merrill.

Rosenthal, R., & Jacobson, L. (1968). *Pygmalion in the classroom.* New York: Holt, Rinehart & Winston.

Rotter, J. (1954). *Social learning and clinical psychology.* Englewood Cliffs, NJ: Prentice Hall.

Rowe, M. B. (1987). Wait-time: Slowing down may be a way of speeding up. *American Educator, 11,* 38-43.

Sabers, D. S., Cushing, K. S., & Berliner, D. C. (1991). Differences among teachers in a task characterized by simultaneity, multidimensionality, and immediacy. *American Educational Research Journal, 28*(1), 63-88.

Shore, S. (1999, April 27). Littleton buries teacher, 3 teens. *San Antonio Express-News,* p. 6A.

Skinner, B. F. (1950). Are theories of learning necessary? *Psychological Review, 57*(4), 193-216.

Skinner, B. F. (1953). *Science and human behavior.* New York: Macmillan.

Skinner, B. F. (1987). *Upon further reflection.* Englewood Cliffs, NJ: Prentice Hall.

Slavin, R. E. (1990). Achievement effects of ability grouping in secondary schools: A best-evidence synthesis. *Review of Educational Research, 6*(3), 471-500.

Slavin, R. E. (1994). *Educational Psychology: Theory and Practice* (4th ed.). Needham Heights, MA: Allyn & Bacon.

Smith, T. (1995). *Findings from the condition of education 1994: America's teachers ten years after the "A Nation at Risk."* (NCES Publication No. 95-766). Washington, DC: U.S. Department of Education.

Smith, T. M., Young, B. A., Bae, Y., Choy, S. P., & Alsalam, N. (1997). *The condition of education 1997.* (NCES Publication 97-388). Washington, DC: U.S. Department of Education.

Snow, R. E., Corno, L., & Jackson III, D. (1996). Individual differences in affective and cognitive functions. In D. Berliner & R. Calfee (Eds.), *Handbook of educational psychology.* New York: Macmillan.

Sprinthall, N., Sprinthall, R., & Oja, S. (1994). *Educational psychology: A developmental approach* (6th ed.). St. Louis, MO: McGraw-Hill.

Stiggins, R. J. (1994). *Student-centered classroom assessment.* Upper Saddle River, NJ: Merrill/Prentice Hall.

Torrance, E. P. (1972). Predictive validity of the Torrance tests of creative thinking. *Journal of Creative Behavior, 6,* 236-232.

Torrey, J. W. (1983). Black children's knowledge of standard English. *American Educational Research Journal, 20*(4), 627-643.

U.S. Department of Education. (1991). *Youth indicators.* Washington, DC: Author.

Vygotsky, L. S. (1993). *The collected works of L. S. Vygotsky: Vol. 2* (J. Knox & C. Stevens, Trans.). New York: Plenum.

Warriner, J., & Griffith, F. (1977). *Warriner's English grammar and composition: Fourth course.* New York: Harcourt Brace Jovanovich.

Weimer, M. (1996). *Improving your classroom teaching.* Thousand Oaks, CA: Sage.

Weiner, B. (1979). A theory of motivation for some classroom experiences. *Journal of Educational Psychology, 71,* 3-25.

Weinstein, C. S. (1996). *Secondary classroom management: Lessons from research and practice.* New York: McGraw-Hill.

Wertsch, J. V. (1991). *Voices of the mind: A sociocultural approach to mediated action.* Cambridge, MA: Harvard University Press.

Wigfield, A., & Eccles, J. S. (1989). Test anxiety in elementary and secondary school students. *Educational Psychologist, 24*(2), 159-183.

Wood, D., Bruner, J., & Ross, G. (1976). The role of tutoring in problem-solving. *Journal of Child Psychology and Allied Disciplines, 17*(2), 89-100.

Woolfolk, A., & Brooks, D. (1983). Nonverbal communication in teaching. *Review of Research in Education, 10,* 103-150.

Woolfolk, A. E. (1998). *Educational psychology* (7th ed.). Boston: Allyn & Bacon.

Index

**CORWIN
PRESS**

The Corwin Press logo—a raven striding across an open book—represents the happy union of courage and learning. We are a professional-level publisher of books and journals for K–12 educators, and we are committed to creating and providing resources that embody these qualities. Corwin's motto is "Success for All Learners."